Mindsight

Colin McGinn

MINDSIGHT

Image, Dream, Meaning

Harvard University Press

Cambridge, Massachusetts, & London, England (2004)

Library of Congress Cataloging-in-Publication Data

McGinn, Colin, 1950–
Mindsight : image, dream, meaning / Colin McGinn.
  p. cm.
Includes bibliographical references and index.
ISBN 0-674-01560-6 (alk. paper)
1. Imagination (Philosophy) I. Title.
B105.I49M36 2004
128'.3—dc22   2004047473

Preface

A few years ago I was sitting contentedly on my porch nursing the blissful feeling that I had run out of ideas. No big projects beckoned, with the accompanying pressure to do the work necessary to complete them. I could lie back, catch up on my reading, pursue my other interests, and take the pressure off—writing books being no kind of picnic. I particularly liked the idea of composing only small essays on subjects I had already written on, with no need to master a new area. Maybe in the remote future I would be struck by something that required a major effort, but for the present all looked calm and relaxed.

The next day, for no particular reason, I found myself thinking about mental images. I made a note or two. It had occurred to me that, contrary to what I had assumed without thinking much about it, images were really very different from perceptions, and in ways that were worth exploring. *Interesting,* I thought (always a fateful moment). I kept coming back to my piece of paper and adding some new observation about the difference. Then I thought I should read something about it. I had never made a study of the literature on imagery, having never really thought about the topic before. Within a few weeks I realized that my earlier bliss had been unfounded: here we go again. Soon I was thinking hard about dreams, and insanity, and meaning—and a book seemed unavoidable. The pressure was on again. (Of course, there was also the pleasure of reclining in the hypnopompic state for hours and calling it work.)

I just found the subject fascinating, and there seemed little current interest in it (compared, say, to consciousness). I found assorted remarks by Wittgenstein and Sartre's *Psychology of Imagination* particularly stimulating (and remarkably similar to each other). The combination of conceptual analysis and phenomenology appealed to me. The subject was also taxing, partly because the phenomenology is so hard to pin down, and partly because imagination is such a far-reaching mental faculty. It is difficult to approach systematically, to impose order on the various manifestations of imagination. That is what I have attempted in this book. My connecting thread throughout is the contrast between imagining and perceiving, and what this precisely consists in.

I would like to be able to thank various grant-awarding bodies and other sources of research time, but in fact I did this work in the interstices of my other regular (and irregular) commitments. It is literally true that it was a full year between my finishing the main text, in the summer of 2002, and my finding the time to write the notes. I have taught the material several times in the course of getting it into shape, notably in a graduate seminar I did with Stephen Neale in 2001. I am grateful to him for stimulating conversations, as well as to the graduate students at Rutgers who attended. Jonathan Miller, Thomas Nagel, and Oliver Sacks provided useful comments. Three outside readers for Harvard University Press produced helpful reports on the initial manuscript. I am also grateful to my wife, Cathy Mortenson, for being a willing subject of my many questions about her images, which are more pronounced than mine.

Contents

Mindsight

Introduction

The topic of imagination is not perhaps as old as imagination itself, but it is pretty old. Plato and Aristotle had their views on imagination, as did the Stoics and Epicureans, and Aquinas and Augustine.[1] Descartes, Locke, Berkeley, Hume, Kant, Fichte, Hegel, and Kierkegaard held opinions on the subject. In the twentieth century, philosophers as diverse as Sartre, Wittgenstein, and Collingwood paid extensive attention to imagination. And very recently cognitive science has come on board to investigate the nature of mental images. Not to mention assorted artists, critics, and psychologists who have weighed in on the topic. Yet contemporary philosophy of mind contains little directly on the imagination, except where it bears on topics such as conceivability and the mind-body problem. Clearly, there is a gap here.

Moreover, imagination has tended to be approached in a fragmentary manner—a little here, a little there—and as part of some larger enterprise. Often there has been an ideological agenda: to advance the cause of empiricism, to show that behaviorism can explain even this most private of mental acts, to demonstrate large claims about the essential creativity of the human soul. Seldom is the topic handled in a comprehensive and impartial manner—simply as a subject of intrinsic interest, with many aspects and varieties. Partly this is because imagination does indeed spread itself widely, making it difficult to achieve a synoptic view. The subject takes in an enormous field—everything from mental images, to dreams and daydreams, to madness, to belief and meaning, to the arts and sciences.

In this book I aim to investigate imagination in as comprehensive a way as possible. I examine it from many angles, employing many methods, and without any particular agenda. It is a phenomenon of the human mind that needs to be analyzed and understood in its own right. It is also elusive, tantalizing, and fascinating. Thinking about it calls for rigor and speculation, clarity and tolerance of obscurity. It positively attracts error and confusion. The study of imagination requires, above all, imagination—and a kind of patient receptivity. Attentiveness to one's own inner life is vital. I shall often call upon my reader to examine his or her imagination as he or she experiences it.

When we think about our mental images we should be struck by two things: (1) how *similar* they are to regular perceptions, and (2) how *different* they are from regular perceptions. Look at the book in front of you; now close your eyes and form an image of it: the two mental episodes will strike you as importantly alike, and yet you won't be in any danger of confusing them. The philosophical task—by no means an easy one—is to explain precisely in what way images and percepts are alike and precisely how they differ. What makes an image an image and a percept a percept? This is the subject of my first chapter, and it is critical to the rest of the book. In it I attempt to characterize the distinction as fully and clearly as I can, drawing on any resources that seem to help—phenomenology, conceptual analysis, and ordinary language. It turns out that, despite the evident affinities between images and percepts, they differ in a number of fundamental respects—so that the Humean view, that images and percepts differ only in degree, is mistaken. Imaging is not a mode of perceiving. This chapter lays the foundation for the rest of the book, in that I employ the distinction between images and percepts throughout my later discussions. Images and percepts are categorically distinct.

Chapter 2 then steps in to restore the balance: visualizing is not the same kind of thing as seeing with one's external eyes, but it is rightly described as *seeing*—with one's mind's eye. Here I defend the view that seeing is a genus with two species—seeing with the body's eye and seeing with the mind's eye. The two species are fundamentally different, yet they are both genuine instances of a more general notion of seeing. Hence my title: *Mindsight*.

Having insisted on the distinctness of images and percepts, I turn in Chapter 3 to a phenomenon in which they come together: seeing-as, or imaginative seeing. I point out what a remarkable phenomenon this is, once the distinction between images and percepts is properly taken to heart. I attempt to clarify seeing-as by invoking the conceptual apparatus developed in Chapter 1, noting its hybrid character.

Chapter 4 takes up the unnerving topic of the "space" of imagery. When I form an image of something, I do not mentally locate it in perceived space; the imagined object presents itself as suspended in its own space. Here again images and percepts differ, yet somewhat mysteriously. The philosophical challenge is to explain what this notion of the space of imagery comes to and how it relates to the space of perception. Images in this regard reach deep obscurity.

In Chapter 5 I address the question of whether images are aptly conceived as internal pictures, viewed with the mind's eye. If we assume that percepts are not themselves pictures we internally view, this would mark a further distinction between images and percepts; I reject the picture theory of images, however, mostly for well-known reasons. More controversially, I interpret recent empirical work that has been supposed to support the picture theory in such a way as not to support that theory. I maintain that putative mental operations such as scanning and inspecting images take as their objects not the image itself, construed as an inner picture, but the thing the image is *of*, which is typically a concrete object (existent or otherwise). Images and percepts are thus alike in both being directed toward external objects ("naïve realism"): we see the same kinds of entity with our mind's eye as with our body's eye.

Next I change gears and move on to dreams. In Chapters 6 and 7 I argue that dreams consist of images, not percepts, and that it is possible to explain dream belief under this hypothesis. Once images and percepts are distinguished, the question of what kind of experience dreams are made of becomes substantive, and by no means easy to answer. And explaining how we can believe what we merely imagine in our dreams requires some far-reaching claims about fiction, suggestibility, and the unconscious.

With dreams under our belt, we can venture into the area of madness. In Chapter 8 my theme is how the image/percept distinction plays out in the understanding of psychotic delusion. My suggestion, not surprisingly, is that the delusions of the insane (like the delusions of the dreamer) are imagination-driven, not perception-driven; the schizophrenic does not, strictly, *hallucinate*.

Chapter 9 enquires speculatively into the origin of imagination in the child, specifically in relation to the way the child forms her beliefs. I suggest that the susceptibility of images to voluntary control plays a crucial part in the child's imaginative maturation.

In Chapter 10 a new phase of the book begins. Advancing from sensory imagining to cognitive imagining, I note various analogies between the two, despite their deep differences, and proceed to discuss how imagination and belief are related. My thesis here is that belief presupposes imagination: beliefs are formed against a background of imaginative mental acts. Imagination is not itself a form of belief but a *sui generis* propositional attitude (as the sensuous image is not a form of percept but a *sui generis* mode of experience). Imagining-that has, indeed, some claim to be the *basic* propositional attitude.

Negation is the topic of Chapter 11, a brief assertion of the relevance of imagination to logic. To negate the actual is to move imaginatively into the realm of modality. Logic is all about the entertaining of possibilities.

Chapter 12 is where the previous two chapters have been leading. I argue that imagination is central to an account of linguistic understanding. To understand a sentence is to imaginatively grasp the possibility it represents. I explain why this is a good way to think about meaning, answering some objections along the way. I use the early Russell and Wittgenstein as foils to explain why we need the imagination to account for meaning. The extreme mentalism of the imagination theory is argued to be a merit of it, not a defect.

Finally, in Chapter 13, I provide a map of the ground we have covered, relating each of the main manifestations of imagination to the others. The idea is to show how the most rudimentary types of imagination might by steps lead to the most sophisticated.

My overall aim is to demonstrate that imagination is a faculty that runs through the most diverse of mental phenomena; it is the theme on which they are variations. We need imagination to have mental images, to dream, to believe, to represent possibilities, and to mean. The imaginative faculty has many expressions and uses. Ubiquitous as it is, however, the mind is not totally shot through with imagination; in particular, ordinary perception is not (unlike seeing-as) inherently imaginative. We have an imaginative side and an unimaginative side—and in this contrast the true character of imagination stands forth. But the imagination, I contend, is a far more pervasive aspect of the human mind than recent philosophy might suggest. If the empiricists took the mind to be essentially a sensing organ, the rationalists a *res cogitans*, recent thinkers a belief/desire preference satisfier, then I would suggest regarding the mind as centrally a device for imagining. We are *Homo imaginans*.[2] It is the mental image and its various elaborations that sums up what the human mind most characteristically is (of course, *all* minds are characterized by consciousness). At any rate, the imagination is a faculty that needs to be accorded a seat of highest honor in any account of human mental nature.

One last point before I begin. The imagination is a topic of considerable interest to people outside analytical philosophy of mind. I am principally an analytical philosopher of mind. I have tried, however, to write in such a way that non-philosophers will be able to follow most of what I am saying, though I would agree that some of what follows is pretty dense. I have confined more technical and esoteric remarks to the notes, as well as references to the (smallish) literature. The subject itself is not technical, though it can certainly be difficult, so the book should be accessible to non-philosophers (at least up to Chapter 10). In particular, the material on dreams is intended to be readable by anyone with an interest in the topic.

I now turn to the seemingly elementary task of distinguishing images and percepts.

Images and Percepts

We are all familiar with the distinction between seeing something and merely visualizing it. If I were in Paris now, I could see the Eiffel Tower; but sitting here in New York I can only visualize it. Seeing requires the presence of the object, while visualizing does not. We do not tend to confuse our images with our percepts. Yet it seems right to characterize both mental operations as *visual*, in the sense that visual experience of some sort is involved; and in both cases the same object—the Eiffel Tower—is the intentional object of my experience. My seeing experience may represent its object as having a certain characteristic shape and color, and will place the object against a certain background; and my visualizing experience may represent the same object as having just that shape, color, and background. So there is a clear similarity between the two types of experience—between their phenomenology, intentionality, and sense-modality—as well as a clear difference.

But what, exactly, is the difference between them? How does the mental act of seeing something differ from that of visualizing something? Generally speaking, we are not ordinarily confused about the distinction—we can tell the difference in our own case—so what is the basis of our ability to differentiate between seeing and visualizing? In other words, how do percepts and images differ?

The classic answer to this question was given by David Hume, at the very beginning of the *Treatise:*

All the perceptions of the human mind resolve themselves into two distinct kinds, which I shall call IMPRESSIONS and IDEAS. The difference betwixt these consists in the degrees of force and liveliness, with which they strike upon the mind, and make their way into our thought or consciousness. Those perceptions, which enter with most force and violence, we may name *impressions;* and under this name I comprehend all our sensations, passions and emotions, as they make their first appearance in the soul. By *ideas* I mean the faint images of these in thinking and reasoning. I believe it will not be very necessary to employ many words in explaining this distinction.[1]

A little later Hume speaks of "the great resemblance between our impressions and ideas in every other particular, except their degree of force and vivacity. The one seems to be in a manner the reflexion of the other; so that all the perceptions of the mind are double, and appear both as impressions and ideas. When I shut my eyes and think of my chamber, the ideas I form are exact representations of the impressions I felt; nor is there any circumstance of the one, which is not to be found in the other."[2] And further on we read: "That idea of red, which we form in the dark, and that impression, which strikes our eyes in sunshine, differ only in degree, not in nature."[3] Given this, it is not surprising to find Hume asserting that "it is not impossible but in particular instances they may very nearly approach to each other. Thus in sleep, in a fever, in madness, or in any very violent emotions of soul, our ideas may approach to our impressions: As on the other hand it sometimes happens, that our impressions are so faint and low, that we cannot distinguish them from our ideas."[4]

According to Hume, then, percepts differ from images merely *quantitatively,* not qualitatively. There is a dimension of variation

along which both images and percepts can be ranged, namely degree of "force and vivacity," so that percepts are simply higher on
this scale than images; hence Hume's claim that images and percepts differ *only* in degree. We might compare this (though Hume
does not) to the different degrees of pain that can be felt, some being more intense than others. The image is merely a faint percept,
just as the percept is a particularly vivid image; both belong together as "perceptions" that can come in various strengths or in-
tensities.[5]

Now, I wish to make two preliminary points about this Humean
conception of the difference between images and percepts before
subjecting it to a sustained critique. First, it is not clear from
Hume's text quite what he means by "force" and "vivacity" and al-
lied locutions. The most natural interpretation (or at least the best
defined) is in terms of the intentional object of the mental act, for
instance, the degree of brightness of the represented object—as
when I see the sun or only visualize it. But a moment's thought
shows the inadequacy of this suggestion, since I can obviously visualize a bright sun and see a dull sun. The degree of brightness of
the intentional *object* is no guide to whether it is being perceived or
visualized; we obviously need to look at the mental act itself, not at
its intentional object. But then what exactly is this notion of "liveliness"? I can certainly entertain an exciting image, just as I can en-
dure a dull and affectless percept. Perhaps Hume has in mind some
idea of the *amount* of consciousness that is taken up respectively by
images and percepts—a little, or a lot. But this is an obscure idea,
and anyway does not seem to deliver the right results, since I can be
very intent on an image and very distracted from a percept. So it is
really not at all clear that the dimension Hume is inviting us to
string images and percepts along is well defined, despite the ease
with which we seem to accept Hume's invitation (and we do seem
curiously prone to be carried along by it). While we can distinguish
within the class of percepts between those that are more vivid than
others—say, in terms of properties of the intentional object—we

cannot use this to distinguish *between* the class of percepts and the class of images; and similarly with respect to distinctions within the class of images. So the availability of a well-defined scale that works within the classes does not provide us with anything that supports Hume's attempt to distinguish between the classes. There is therefore an obscurity at the very heart of Hume's criterion, even aside from its necessity or sufficiency. Perhaps this obscurity could be fixed up, but my preliminary point is that the question is by no means trivial.[6]

Second, Hume himself tacitly concedes the inadequacy of his criterion, without batting much of an eyelid over it. For he allows that images can be as forceful as percepts in dreams, fever, and madness; and he also allows that percepts can on occasion be as faint as images. This means, of course, that "degree of vivacity" (whatever exactly that is) is neither necessary nor sufficient to distinguish images from percepts. Faintness is not a necessary condition for being an image because of dreams, fever, and madness; and it is not sufficient either because of very faint percepts. Undeterred by this, however, Hume persists in his conviction that in the majority of cases his quantitative criterion works well enough. He shows no awareness that he must be tacitly operating with some *other* criterion even to state his own counterexamples: he must have some distinct reason for declaring dreams to consist of images, not percepts, and some other conception in order to declare that faint percepts don't count as images. Presumably this cannot simply be that percepts have existent objects while images do not, since that is hardly necessarily true: there are clearly such things as perceptual hallucinations, and we can form images of real objects. The difference must be *intrinsic*, not a matter of whether there exists a corresponding object. So Hume has a serious problem here. He begins by saying his criterion is so obvious as not to need much commentary, and within a page has admitted that it is false.[7]

No doubt Hume is influenced here by the phenomenon of the

memory image: such images can seem like decayed versions of the earlier percept from which they are derived. I shall be discussing memory images at length later, but for now I simply note that this admitted derivational relationship does not imply the faint percept conception of the image. We can agree that the memory image is some kind of remnant or echo or re-presentation of the original percept (and is causally dependent on it) without accepting that the image is merely a fainter version of the percept. Image and percept could differ in other ways (perhaps qualitatively or in "nature") and it still be true that the image derives from an antecedent percept. Indeed, there is no logical reason why a memory image cannot be derived from a percept and be *more* vivid than the percept (again, whatever precisely the favored notion of vividness might be).

The essence of Hume's conception is that an image is really a type of percept—merely a sickly or degraded percept, a percept drained of its usual pungency, a decayed and etiolated percept, but a percept nonetheless. An image is like a percept, he says, in every respect save its "vivacity." I shall now argue that this is a fundamental mistake; there are a number of important respects in which images differ markedly from percepts. We shall see that percepts, whether veridical or hallucinatory, no matter what their degree of "vivacity," belong on one side of a line (along with after-images), while mental images proper belong on the other side. Despite the initial attraction of Hume's theory, he could hardly be more wrong (though he was perfectly right to insist on the deep *similarity* between percepts and images). Since we are prone to slide so easily into line with Hume when we first encounter his formulations, I think this is one of those cases in which we are naturally disposed to misunderstand and oversimplify our own concepts—and so a textbook example of Wittgenstein's general account of philosophical error. We seem eager to make mistaken conceptual assimilations when it comes to images.[8]

Not surprisingly, then, we find Wittgenstein taking a keen (if truncated) interest in the topic of imagery. In a condensed but highly suggestive passage, he writes:

> Auditory images, visual images—how are they distinguished from sensations? Not by "vivacity."
> Images tell us nothing, either right or wrong, about the external world. (Images are not hallucinations, nor yet fancies).
> While I am looking at an object I cannot imagine it.
> Difference between the language-games: "Look at this figure!" and "Imagine this figure!"
> Images are subject to the will.
> Images are not pictures. I do not tell what object I am imagining by the resemblance between it and the image.
> Asked "What image have you?" one can answer with a picture.[9]

I take this as my text in delineating the features that distinguish images from percepts, as follows.

1. The Will

Perhaps the most obvious difference between images and percepts is that images can be willed but percepts cannot. I can set myself to form an image of the Eiffel Tower now and carry out my intention, but I cannot simply decide to *see* the Eiffel Tower. This asymmetry applies as much to weak percepts as it does to vivid ones; percepts do not become voluntary simply by diminishing in vivacity. Nor is this voluntariness a matter of degree—with vivid percepts being less voluntary than faint ones. So Hume is wrong that the difference between images and percepts is *merely* a matter of degree. Wittgenstein writes: "We do not 'banish' visual impressions, as we do images. And we don't say of the former, either, that we might *not* banish them."[10] Also: "The concept of imaging is rather like one of doing than receiving. Imagining might be called a creative act. (And is of course so called)."[11] We might put this point by saying that "visualize" is a verb of action while "see" is not—which is why it makes sense to command someone to visualize something but not to command him to see something. Preserving an image in consciousness can also require a good deal of mental *effort*, while there is no effort involved in the sustaining of a percept; that job is out of one's hands, so to speak. Forming an image is something I *do*, while seeing is something that happens to me; in short, imaging is a mental action.

This simple formulation seems to me to be essentially correct, but we need to make some qualifications if it is not to be open to counterexamples. First, and most obvious, the claim has to be that imaging is a *basic* action while seeing is not, in the sense that it can be brought about without doing anything else. Of course, I can decide to see something if that is taken to mean that I can perform some actions as a result of which I have a perceptual experience: I can go to Paris and have a look at the Eiffel Tower, thus seeing it. But what I cannot do is simply will myself to have such an experience without undertaking any means-end actions. I can also decide to believe, if that means undertaking a course of action the result of which is that I believe something; but this does not imply that I can *directly* decide to believe.[12] In the case of imaging, however, I can simply directly decide to form an image of something. Imaging is like *looking* in this respect, and unlike seeing.[13]

Second, the claim should not be that every case of forming an image is fully voluntary. It is a familiar experience to find oneself compulsively imagining certain things, for images to come unbidden, for images to resist the effort to eliminate them. The point cannot then be that every occurrence of an image is a free action that one is at liberty to refrain from. Rather, the point is that it makes *sense* to try to control one's images, even when one cannot. But this kind of involuntariness mirrors exactly what we find with compulsive action generally—for example, obsessive hand washing. That an action is compulsive does not show that it is not an action, nor even that it is not intentional; it is still something that one *does*.

The essential point is that compulsive actions are still "subject to the will" (in Wittgenstein's phrase) in that it makes sense to direct the will at them, and the will can influence their course and character.

It is helpful here to distinguish three points at which images are subject to the will: their inception, their course, and their termination. In most cases the image is subject to the will at all three points: we can decide when to have them, we can decide how they will change over time, and we can decide when they will end. But in some cases the image just "pops into the mind" and so is not willed at its inception; yet it is typically subject to the will in its course, as well as in its termination (sexual fantasies are an obvious example). And even when the image is resistant to the will in all three phases, it is still in principle subject to it—though this may require greater effort, or more self-discipline, or even a course of training (or therapy). Imagery is as much prone to weakness of the will as bodily action, and shows as many varieties of *akrasia* as bodily action. In fact, the same kinds of distinctions and qualifications that need to be made in the general philosophy of action apply also in this case of mental action.[14]

Third, there are the cases of images that are not compulsive or the result of weakness of will but that simply populate consciousness in a kind of random, unfocused, unplanned manner—the sort you hardly notice but which provide a kind of background hum of imagistic activity. These I would compare to the small bodily movements that we engage in without planning or even intending them: the drumming of the fingers, twitching of the feet, and rolling of the tongue that so often accompany (say) the act of reading. These are the kinds of actions Brian O'Shaughnessy dubbed "subintentional" and which form an important subclass of human actions.[15] My point is that these bodily subintentional actions have their counterpart in the realm of mental actions—as images flit across one's mind in a kind of low-level play of mental activity. These are subject to the will in the sense that I *can* focus on them and shape their comings and goings, though typically I pay little heed to them; just as I can decide to stop drumming my fingers as I read.

In the above respects imagery mirrors thought. Thinking, too, is subject to the will in all the complex ways I have just gestured at; but this complexity should not make us doubt the intuitive first thought that thinking is a mental action—as opposed to perceiving, which takes place outside the scope of the will. Just as thinking differs from perceiving in respect of its voluntariness, so does imagining; indeed, it is natural to suspect that (as we shall see) there is a close connection here—that thinking and imagining are of a piece.

Subjection to the will implies a difference in the *causation* of images and percepts. Percepts typically have their causal origin in external stimuli; and even in the case of total hallucination, the causation does not involve the subject's decision-making mechanisms (it may simply involve implanted electrodes or some such). But in the case of images, the causation comes from "inside"; it is endogenous, not exogenous. It is very tempting to resort to the idiom of agent causation here: it is *I* who cause the mental images that occupy my consciousness. But it is certainly not the case that I cause my perceptual experiences. Of course, a weak percept is no more caused by me than a strong one is—so the Humean theory misses this structural difference in causal background. If the correct theory of action, however, is that desires cause actions (along with other mental states such as beliefs and intentions), then we can say the same for the action of forming an image; but again, it would be quite wrong to say that perceptions are caused by desires and the like. The will has no causal control over what you see and hear.[16]

Now, much more could be said about imagery and the philosophy of action—and I think it would be a very worthwhile project to explore this topic more fully—but my purpose here is just to identify the *differentia* that mark images off from percepts, so I won't pursue the topic of the philosophy of mental (specifically, imagistic) action further. I take it I have said enough to indicate that images and percepts are asymmetrically related to the will, and that this is an important difference between them.[17] Imagining belongs to the active part of our nature, perceiving belongs to the passive part; imagining is a product of our faculties of spontaneity, perceiving a product of our faculties of receptivity (to employ Kantian terminology). This is something for which the Humean conception finds no place: for Hume, the image is assumed to be a passively received version of an earlier percept, not something that belongs to the category of action.

Three brief points remain to be made in this section. The first concerns the epistemology of the image/percept distinction—that is, how we tell them apart in our own case. According to Hume, we introspectively detect the gradations of vividness our "perceptions" display and judge accordingly; we notice the faintness and categorize the experience as imagistic. But once we recognize that images are active and percepts passive, we have another account of how we tell the difference: we are aware that the will is involved in the one case and not the other. We are aware of our own acts of will and their products, and we can sort our mental states by this standard. In other words, the will is involved in the first-person epistemology of image judgments.[18]

Second, there is a delicate question about the relation between the willed nature of images and their intrinsic experiential character. To say that images are *produced* by the will is not yet to say that their internal phenomenology differs from that of percepts; and couldn't there be mental items that were phenomenologically just like percepts and yet were as subject to the will as our mental images? This does not seem conceptually excluded, and yet there does seem to be some sense in which the phenomenology of images is affected by their voluntariness: what it is like to have them seems affected by the fact that they are products of will; their causation is somehow imprinted on their phenomenology.[19] Nevertheless, strictly speaking, the productive history of the image is extrinsic to it, since it relates to the causation of the image. In contrast to some of the other characteristic features of images I shall consider later, their voluntariness is not internal to their intentionality—to how they represent their intentional objects. So what it is like to have an image incorporates the fact that images are subject to the will, but this character of consciousness does not intrude on the intentional properties of the image.

Third, there is a large and important class of apparent exceptions to the voluntariness condition, which cannot be dismissed in the way I dismissed some other alleged counterexamples: namely, dream experiences. If dream experiences are imagistic, how can subjection to the will be a necessary condition of being an image, since dreams are not, on the face of it, voluntarily chosen; we seem passive before their onslaught. This is a serious question, which I shall address fully later; for now I am simply alerting the reader to this potential objection to what I have said so far. Of course, if dreams are *not* imagistic, but consist of percepts, there is not even a prima facie problem; but, as we shall see, there is good reason to reject this suggestion.

2. Observation

Wittgenstein says, "Images tell us nothing, either right or wrong, about the external world."[20] Later he adds, "It is just because forming images is a voluntary activity that it does not instruct us about the external world."[21] In the same vein he expands on this thought: "When we form an image of something we are not observing. The coming and going of the pictures is not something that *happens* to us. We are not surprised by these pictures, saying 'Look!' (Contrast with e.g. after-images)."[22] We find a strikingly similar expression of the same idea in Sartre's *Psychology of Imagination:* "The image teaches nothing: it is organized exactly like the objects which do produce knowledge, but it is complete at the very moment of its appearance. If I amuse myself by turning over in my mind the image of a cube, if I pretend that I see its different sides, I shall be no further ahead at the close of the process than I was at the beginning: I have learned nothing."[23] A little later: "No matter how long I may look at an image, I shall never find anything in it but what I put there. It is in this fact that we find the distinction between an image and a perception."[24] Finally: "The image teaches nothing, never produces an impression of novelty, and never reveals any new aspect of the object. It delivers it in a lump. No risk, no anticipation: only a certainty. My perception can deceive me, but not my image. Our attitude toward the object of the image could be called 'quasi-observation.'"[25]

Let us summarize these remarks by saying simply that images are not *informative*, while percepts are. And the reason for this is that the image contains only what I myself have put into it: I decide to form an image of a red cube, and do so; the image thus contains precisely what I intended to bestow upon it.[26] I no more learn from images than I learn from the sentences I write down, since in both cases I merely express my antecedent intention. But when I am seeing external objects, I am flooded with information whose causal origin is not me and my intentions but an independent objective world whose properties are being revealed to me. Accordingly, I adopt a totally different attitude toward the object of my image and the object of my percept: in the latter case I adopt an attitude of observation; in the former I do not. Thus I may strain my eyes, fix my attention on a particular portion of my visual field, diligently examine the object in question; I make myself open to what the object imparts to me. In this dynamic process I continually update my beliefs about the object, adding new beliefs, perhaps rejecting some earlier belief. Perception is an informational channel, and the percept is its vehicle. But when I form an image, I do not strain my eyes and focus on a portion of my visual field; indeed, I may close my eyes and let my attention wander from the world around me. The object of my imaging does not feed new information to me as I image it, and there is no updating of my beliefs about its properties. I do not adopt an attitude of cognitive openness to what the object might reveal about itself; there is no dynamic flow of information from it to me—just a static positing of the object, which is causally remote from my current mental activity. There is no observational *input* from the object. Hence the lack of surprise occasioned by the image. We do not have an attitude of ignorant expectancy toward the future behavior of our imaged objects—because they are our created creatures. They tell us nothing we do not already know.

None of this is compatible with the Humean conception: a faint percept is still something that mediates the observational attitude. If Hume were right, we would be intent on receiving information from the external world during acts of imaging; but of course we are not. Our cognitive relation to our images is totally different from our cognitive relation to our percepts. We know that the causal source of images is not the impact of the external world but our own acts of will, so we do not find ourselves eager to gather more information about an external stimulus. But the mere faintness of a percept could not possibly produce this attitude of indifference in us; it might make us try even harder to pick up signals from the outside.

Now, I think that all of this is basically right, but the formulations given by Sartre and Wittgenstein are open to objection; so we will need to tighten them up a bit, removing an element of overstatement in them. Both writers assert baldly that we can learn nothing from the image—that it reflects prior knowledge rather than produces new knowledge. But recent work in cognitive science seems to refute this unqualified assertion of what Sartre calls "the poverty of the image."[27] Suppose you ask subjects whether the navel is above the waistline or whether frogs have lips. Many people report forming an image and reading the answer off that image. Without forming the image, they may be at a loss for a reply; but with it they can supply the answer. Thus the image seems to augment their knowledge. What is going on here? Clearly they conjure up a memory image, derived from past perceptions, and extract the information from this. So their knowledge base is enriched by employing the image. Information is encoded in the image in one sort of form (often described as pictorial), and then it is transformed into another sort of informational encoding—the kind that corresponds to articulate beliefs. So there is some kind of cognitive enhancement occasioned by the image; something is learned.

Does this undermine the kind of contrast Wittgenstein and Sartre are trying to bring out? No, because their point had to do with the particular *way* that percepts inform and images do not: they are speaking of the *flow* of information from object to belief system and the associated attitude of observation—and this contrast still holds once we concede the way that images *can* inform us. Compare the way that we can achieve cognitive advances by the procedure of making explicit what was previously implicit, as when we spell out the logical consequences of our beliefs. Clearly, reasoning of this sort can lead to new knowledge, but just as clearly it does not involve observation and informational flow from the object. In the same way, I suggest, the conversion of information stored in the memory in image form into information stored in the form of explicit knowledge does not involve observation and information flow. It is quite true that the content of such images is not exhausted by what the subject intentionally injects into the image from his stock of knowledge, so Wittgenstein and Sartre exaggerate when they suggest otherwise; but their basic point still survives, because there is no new information coming from the object into our informational systems in these cases. The information is already stored in memory; what happens is simply that it is converted into another form. The content of the memory image came from the object originally, but the cognitive transition does not involve any *further* information from the object; it is restricted to what memory already contains. And in this respect there is still a stark contrast with perception. The simple point is that the image is not being continuously updated by the object, as the dynamic flow of perception updates one's percepts; after all, the imagined object is typically elsewhere, not in contact with us at all. It is not in a position to feed new information into our cognitive system.[28]

I would make a further point. There is a clear sense in which percepts *invite* belief, even if the invitation is resisted because of conflicting knowledge—as when you have good reason to believe you are hallucinating. Percepts supply (defeasible) reasons to believe; they insist on their own veracity. But images do not invite belief in this way; they do not *purport* to tell us how the world is. They are neutral about reality. If they are to have any reality-affirming force, we must *take* them to be veridical. But in the typical case we have no tendency to believe what our images represent: if I form an image of a tiger in my room, I am under no impulsion to believe there is a tiger in my room. On the contrary, since it is an *image* that is in my consciousness, I know very well that this is no reason to believe in the presence of a tiger.[29] Not only does the image not tell us about the external world in the way the percept does; it does not even try to: it is not in this line of business. The image is not evidence that things are presently thus-and-so in the external world, since we can conjure it up at will. If I ask you to form an image, I am not inviting you to believe that things are as you (merely) imagine. It is, indeed, irrational to believe what you merely imagine, whereas believing what you perceive is the soul of rationality. Percepts *entitle* you to form the corresponding belief, but images do not. And again, this point is incompatible with the Humean view that images are simply degraded percepts, which are evidential in character.

Finally, I have to mention a potential counterexample to the claims of this section: dreams. In dreams we do seem to form new beliefs at the invitation of our experience, so the dream seems to resemble the flow of perception over time. Thus if dreams consist of images, then some images appear to be belief-inviting. There certainly seem to be surprises occasioned by the content of dreams.

Again, I will reply to this when I come to consider dreams in their own right.

3. Visual Field

The human visual field has certain well-known characteristics, which I shall merely list here. It has a boundary or perimeter, a center and a periphery, a blind spot; it presents objects as in some definite spatial relation to the perceiver; it exhibits depth, aided by binocularity; it permits concentration on parts of it ("foveation"); it presents objects in a foreground/background configuration; it can be eliminated by closing the eyelid. These features are imposed by the anatomy and physiology of the eye, particularly the retina, as they interact with the laws of optics. What is in your visual field is obviously constrained by whether the object can emit light rays that impinge upon the cells of the retina. When we speak of how much of the visual field is occupied by a particular object, we are speaking of how much of the retina is devoted to processing light from that object. The eye is a psychophysical system par excellence. And note that no matter how degraded and "faint" a percept may become, it still occurs with a fully constituted visual field.

But none of this holds of images. There is no boundary to the image imposed by the constraints of optics and retinal anatomy, so we do not have the experience of taking in new imaged objects as we shift the orientation of the inner eye: we do not *point* the inner eye in a new direction when we form a new image, rotating it in some intracerebral socket. It is not that an internal retina is irradiated by the light from the new object of imagining. Nor is there a distinction between the center of the image and its periphery, with attention concentrated at the center; the entire image is equally central (I shall say more about this later when I come to consider the role of attention). Obviously, there is no blind spot, caused by the origin of the optic nerve from the retina to the brain. The imaged object is not presented as in some definite spatial relation to the perceiver—that is, typically, in front of him.[30] The content of the image does not inform us as to where the object is in perceiver-centered space. Such depth as the image contains is not owed to the effects of binocular disparity (again, I shall return later to the question of how *many* inner eyes we can be said to have). Such foreground/background configuration as the image has is not a function of the actual spatial layout of the objects in relation to the perceiver's body. There is no eyelid for the inner eye that works by blocking light and hence interrupting the image.

I can summarize all this by saying that the visual field of the body's eye is deeply connected to the facts of sensory anatomy and physics, but the image is under no such constraints. This is why we can imagine what has no privileged spatial relation to the body. The intuitive manifestation of this is that perceived objects are felt to be in a definite relation to the bodily eyes—they are arrayed before them in a spatial manifold—but the inner eye does not present its objects as in any such relation to the body. There is a temptation to say that the visual percept occurs at the psychic periphery, where the mind makes its contact with the external world, while the image occurs "further back," in the inner recesses of the mind (nearer to thought, perhaps), and does not link us directly to the world outside. But this way of putting it, however intuitive (even poetic), should, I think, be taken to be just a colorful way to put the point about the visual field that I am laboring.

One further observation needs to be made about space and the visual field. Not only does the visual field present objects as in spatial relation to the perceiver, but also it presents them as in spatial relation to one another. There is no such thing as the isolated object of perception; the visual field demands to be filled—even if only by empty space. Visual intentionality is necessarily multiple or inclusive; it takes in what is present in the ambient stimulus. But imagery can detach an object from its surroundings and posit it alone: when I form an image of the Eiffel Tower, I don't have to include the buildings behind it or the plane flying over it. The image is selective, abstracting, punctate. True, I cannot form an image of something without also imaging at least some of its parts, but I don't have to image any other object. The visual field compels me to see what is present in it, but in the image I can choose what to include; I am not at the mercy of the energy emitted by the objects around me. Again, this is a feature that the Humean conception cannot acknowledge, since even weak percepts have their visual field of multiply presented objects (even if it is just the blackness of night).[31]

A final point: the eye or the ear can be flooded with energy, causing discomfort (or worse) and breakdown of function. Thus we can be blinded by the light or deafened by the volume: too much energy at the receptors, resulting in temporary or permanent damage. But there is no analogue of this in the realm of imagery: the inner eye cannot be blinded by light and the inner ear cannot be deafened by sound. No matter how bright the sun you imagine or how loud the tune you hear "in your head," you will suffer no damage and feel no discomfort. For once Hume's theory can accommodate this, since a faint percept cannot blind or deafen; but I take it that this is a merely fortuitous theoretical success. Better to say that the image is just not the *kind* of thing that can be overloaded in the way the senses can be. The image is simply not in the grip of the physics of the object in the way the percept is. The psychology of the image is not physically constrained in the same way the psychology of the percept is (which is not to say, of course, that it operates under *no* physical constraints; it clearly depends on the operation of suitable brain mechanisms).

To say that the visual image has no visual field is not, of course, to say that the notion of *expanse* has no application to the image—I think it does—but it is to say that this notion is not some sort of duplication for the inner eye of the visual field of the outer eye, with its distinctive characteristics. Visual imagery indeed represents in a spatial mode, but it does not do so by embedding the spatiality of its objects within the kind of visual field constitutive of the visual

percept (I shall have more to say about what the phenomenal similarity between images and percepts does consist in later).

4. Indeterminacy and Saturation

It has been very widely noted that images can be indeterminate,
perhaps necessarily so.[32] My image of a hen, say, may not represent
it as having any particular number of speckles; my image of J. F.
Kennedy may not specify his eye color. The thought here is that the
image leaves open certain facts about its object, and if there is no
real object, then there will be no fact of the matter about certain
features of the object. The image is like a story in this respect: it is
constitutionally incomplete. I think this familiar point is perfectly
correct, but it is less obvious that it provides a clear contrast with
percepts, at least if understood as a radical difference in nature. My
percept may also be incomplete with respect to certain properties
of its object, say, if I am too far away from a person to register her
eye color. Suppose I hallucinate a hen: is it so clear that my percept
attributes a definite number of speckles to the nonexistent hen? Of
course, real objects themselves are determinate, but they can be
imagined too. The question is whether the representational state is
complete in certain respects: does it settle all questions about what
it represents? In neither image nor percept does the answer appear
to be affirmative. Maybe images are typically *more* indeterminate
than percepts, but both seem to admit of some indeterminacy; if
so, there is no ground for a sharp distinction here.

I think there is, however, a closely related property that does
mark a sharp distinction (and maybe some authors have conflated
indeterminacy with this)—which I shall call *saturation*. The idea is
this: every point of the visual field is such that some quality is manifest there, whereas this is not true of the image. The percept represents the world as dense, filled, continuous; but the image is gappy,
coarse, discrete. I am speaking phenomenologically here: at every
point of the phenomenal visual field you can find a manifested

quality (even if that quality is on the borderline between two other qualities), but in the image there are points at which nothing is manifested—not even an indeterminate quality. I form an image of my mother's face, but there are many points at which my image is utterly silent; I just select certain features as sufficient to make it an image of my mother, and I leave the rest blank. But if I see my mother's face, there is no blank anywhere—there is phenomenal plenitude. The physical stimulus does the work of filling everything in as it interacts with my sensory system, but in the case of the image, the content has to come from my own resources—and they may be insufficient to plug up every gap. Thus the percept is saturated and the image unsaturated; in this sense, there is a special "poverty" in the image, to use Sartre's term. This notion is difficult to make rigorous and precise (what isn't in this area?),[33] but I think it has enough intuitive force to be added to our list of *differentia*.

5. *Attention*

Percepts and images relate very differently to the faculty of attention. I can pay attention to what I am seeing or I can fail to pay attention to it; but I do not have this choice in the case of images: here I must pay attention in order to be imaging at all. Consider the well-known case of the truck driver whose mind is wandering from the road: he is not paying attention to what he is seeing—because his attention is focused on the dinner he will be eating when he gets home—and yet he still has visual experience.[34] The existence of the percept does not depend on directing attention to what the percept is of. Similarly, if you focus your attention on a portion of your visual field, the rest does not disappear; it hovers unattended. And you can shift your attention back to the unattended portion without thereby producing it anew. Clearly, you can enjoy sensory experiences from each of your sense-modalities simultaneously and not be attending to all of them. Percepts provide what we might call "pre-attentive intentionality": that is, they can exist and represent and be conscious, without the kind of intentional directedness that comes with attention. Referring with words seems necessarily a case of attentive intentionality (as does the intentionality of occurrent thoughts), but the intentionality of percepts is not essentially attentive (though it is conscious, in one clear sense). Your perception can be *of* something you are not then attending to.[35]

Now, what I want to claim is that images necessarily involve attentive intentionality, and I will put this by saying that they are "attention-dependent." The claim here is not that one has to attend to the image itself in order for it to exist (the analogue of attending to the words you utter when you refer to objects); the claim is rather that one has to attend to the *object* of the image in order for the image to exist. In order to form and sustain an image of my mother, I must be attending to my mother—that is, thinking about her in an attentive manner (but I don't have to direct my attention in this way in order merely to *see* her, as opposed to *look* at her). To attend to my *image* of her would be another attentive act altogether, and not an act I need necessarily to perform in order to form the appropriate image.

To see this, we can ask whether there are analogues for images of the cases I just cited to show that percepts are not attention-dependent. Suppose our truck driver switches his attention back to the road and away from his imagined dinner: do his dinner images survive this shift? I think the obvious answer is no. They no more survive this shift than his dinner thoughts do. Nothing sustains the images but his attention, while in the case of the perceived road, there is the ongoing impact of the road on his visual system. Look at something in front of you, then form an image of your mother; your percept survives in unattended form. Now switch attention back to the seen object while trying to keep your mother image; you won't succeed. Or again, try to focus on part of an image while keeping the rest intact; the best you can do is replace the first image with an image of the part in question. Or, finally, try to form a visual image and an auditory image simultaneously; I think you will either find this to be impossible or find that you have to divide your attention to do it. But that is not what happens when you have visual and auditory percepts together; no division of attention is necessary in order to bring off this feat—indeed, it is not a *feat* at all. It requires no effort, no forced division of attention. But images are greedy for attention; it is what they live off. Again, this does not fit the Humean view, since weak percepts are as attention-independent as strong ones.

It is this that lies behind the fact that there can be unnoticed aspects of what is being perceived but not of what is being imagined. Since I do not (could not?) pay attention to everything in my visual field, there are aspects of the way I see things that I fail to notice: I see much more than I can report or than I can commit to memory.[36] I don't notice, say, the color of a flower worn in someone's buttonhole, though I certainly saw the color: it registered in my visual field.[37] But nothing like this can hold for images; there are no aspects of them that I fail to notice. Since they are attention-dependent, their features are given to the attentive faculties, and so cannot escape detection. But because attention is selective, images will not have the kind of detail found in percepts—hence their lack of saturation. There will be many details of the percept that are not noticed, but the image can have only such detail as is noticed. In other words, since attention is more restricted than perception, images will have a comparably impoverished content. It is as if the image can contain only so much of the content of a percept as can be attended to, and this is a relatively small part of the total content of the percept. But it is not the *amount* of detail that is crucial; it is the fact that the detail is attention-dependent that marks the image off from the percept. We might say that the image is *created* by the act of attention, while the percept is generated by an outside stimulus.

This attention-dependence connects with subjection to the will. For attention is itself an active faculty, a matter of deploying the will: you decide what you will attend to—or at least this is always in principle possible. Looking at something is active, even if seeing is not; and looking is an act of attention. When I voluntarily form an image, I am voluntarily directing my attention in a certain way; but merely seeing something does not in itself require any direction of attention. We might say that *because* images are attention-dependent, they are subject to the will. To banish an image, say, is to cease to attend to its object in the imagistic mode. And an object cannot become an object of imagination unless it is attended to (in the imaginative mode); so forming an image is just an act of attending imaginatively. In this respect imaging is like thinking: it is also true that you cannot think about something you are not paying attention to. And the voluntariness of thinking is also inextricably connected to its essentially attentive character. So it may be that the attention-dependence of images underlies and explains their subjection to the will; in any case, the two are inextricably intertwined.

6. Absence

This point is implicit in what I said about the visual field, but it is worth bringing it out separately. Sartre writes: "It is of the very nature of my image of [Peter] not to touch him or see him, a way he has *of not being* at such a distance, in such a position. The characteristic of Peter is . . . to be 'intuitive-absent,' given to intuition as absent."[38] Thus: "The characteristic of the intentional object of the imaginative consciousness is that the object is not present and is posited as such, or that it does not exist and is posited as not existing, or that it is not posited at all." Sartre's thought here is that the percept "posits" its object as existing and present (even when it is a hallucination), but the image "posits" its object as absent or not existing. This difference shows that the image cannot be a type of percept, no matter how faint, since all percepts imply presence.

Now, I think this is a sound observation, but I want to refine it a little. It is obvious that not all objects of sight are *near* to the perceiver; some are millions of miles away, such as the stars. And this spatial remoteness can be part of how the percept represents the world. So in one sense the percept can represent an object that is absent from the perceiver. But I take it this is not a serious objection to Sartre's point: his point is that the percept includes a specification of spatial relatedness as between perceiver and object, even when the object is very distant. The image, by contrast, is *neutral* about spatial relatedness; it does not specify any particular spatial relation to the perceiver's body. When I form an image of Peter, I may have no spatial information about his whereabouts of any kind. Nor need I have any information about his spatial relation to other things—as I do when I see Peter. We can put this by saying that perceptual consciousness contains a kind of double reference—to the object and to the perceiver's body—while the imaginative consciousness makes no such reference; it simply posits its object in a way that is neutral about its relation to the imaginer's body. So, in a sense, perception presupposes an embodied consciousness in a way that imagination does not. The "absence" of the imagined object is an indication that the body has been "transcended" in imagination; that is, no definite relation between object and body is implicated in the intentionality of the imaginative consciousness. Embodiment and subject-location are essential to perception, but they are not part of the intrinsic character of the imaginative act; they are not constitutive of its intentional content (this is not to say that they might not be essential in some other way). The "absence" of which Sartre speaks could as well be described as the absence of the body from imaginative intentionality, in contrast to the presence of the body in all perception.[39]

7. Recognition

It has been very widely noted that the identity of one's imaginative object enjoys epistemic privileges. Sartre puts the point forthrightly: "When I say: 'the object I perceive is a cube,' I make an hypothesis that I may have to reject at the close of my perceptions. When I say: 'the object of which I have an image at this moment is a cube,' my judgment is final: it is absolutely certain that the object of my image is a cube."[40] That is, I cannot misidentify the object of my imagining. I have no wish to labor this familiar point, but I do want to provide a different way of formulating it which I think brings out the underlying asymmetry. The reason for the asymmetry is clearly that the identity of my imagined object is fixed by my imaginative intentions, to which I have special access, while the identity of the perceived object is fixed by what is out there in the external world, and I have no special access to this. In the one case the intentional object is *stipulated*, in the other it is not.

It is because of this that no act of *recognition* is required in the image case, while it is for the perception case. Abstractly put, the mechanism of perceptual recognition contains two moments or phases: first, sensory information is received as the appearance of the object is registered; second, an identity judgment is invoked of the form "the object that has such-and-such an appearance is identical to A." Then the subject judges that the seen object, which has such-and-such an appearance, is A—that is, she makes a suitable recognitional judgment. But in the case of the image there is no such process: it is *not* that an appearance is registered in the image and then an appropriate identity judgment is made based on information stored in memory; there *is* no such inference from appearance to object identity. The identity of the object is epistemically prior to its appearance in the image: the imaginer starts with the object and then constructs an image of it. He does not have to figure out the identity of the object from the way his image represents it. The object is *given*, not inferred. I know that my image is of my mother because I *intended* it to be; I don't have to consult the appearance of the person in the image and then infer that I must have formed an image of my mother.[41] This is why our knowledge of the identity of our imaginative objects is not recognitional knowledge, with all the pitfalls associated with such knowledge. And again, this fact sits ill with the Humean conception of images; indeed, a weak percept would seem particularly prone to errors of identification. If I have a faint percept of someone with some of the appearance of my mother, I can easily mis-recognize whom I am seeing; it might just be the somewhat similar lady who lives next door. In imagery, by contrast, no act of recognition occurs at all—any more than it does when I simply decide to *think* about my mother. And where there is no recognition, there is no possibility of recognitional error.

8. Thought

Seeing X does not stop you from thinking about Y. You can be staring at a blue ocean and thinking of your beloved. This is because the perceptual act does not require your full attention (or indeed any of it); your mind is thus free to wander from what you are seeing without your going instantly blind. Seeing and thinking are not in competition for attentional resources (unlike *looking* and thinking). But the matter is quite otherwise for imaging and thinking: here I venture to suggest that you cannot form an image of X and simultaneously think of Y. Once your thoughts wander from X to Y, your image of X ceases to be. Of course, if the image were merely a faint percept, there would be no reason for this to be so; the faintness should make it *easier* for your thoughts to move elsewhere. I think the reason for this tie between thought and image should be obvious, given what I said earlier: since images are attention-dependent, letting your attention wander to other matters will eliminate the image. It is like trying to have two thoughts at the same time. (This might encourage the idea that an image *is* a thought; I discuss this later on.) So imagining X and thinking of Y do compete for resources. This, then, is another respect in which images and percepts differ in basic nature: percepts allow thought to range freely, but images constrain thought.[42]

9. Occlusion

Here is a very familiar fact about percepts and images: you can have images at the same time that you have percepts (at least where image and percept are of different things). I can be seeing a chair and having an image of an apple. In such a case it would be quite wrong to say that my image *interferes* with my percept—though it does recruit attention away from what I am seeing. I am not in any sense *blinded* by my image. Let us express this by saying that the image is "non-occlusive." The image does not block my sensory systems or cause them to malfunction or even distort the phenomenal character of my percept; image and percept happily coexist. Contrast this with the way after-images affect my perceptual state: here I am partially blinded to what is in front of me; the after-image does occupy part of my visual field; it does alter the phenomenal character of my percepts. It is occlusive. The after-image belongs to the same system as the percept, competing for its resources, while the image proper is extrinsic to this system. And what holds of after-images holds *a fortiori* of percepts themselves: they are occlusive. If I am hallucinating X, this will certainly interfere with my perception of Y, wholly or partially. Drug-induced hallucinations, such as those caused by LSD, do affect the visual field in pronounced ways; they compete with ordinary visual perception. You cannot see something as red and simultaneously see it as green (all over etc.), but you can see it as red and *imagine* it as green. One of the most important characteristics of imagination is precisely that it enables you to picture the world in other ways than it is represented in perception.

This point again gives the lie to the Humean conception, since weak percepts are occlusive, just like weak after-images; they occupy the visual system and force out other potential percepts. But images don't work like this: they reside in a separate system, competing with other images to be sure, but not with percepts. Accordingly, one way to test whether a given type of experience is perceptual or imagistic is to ask whether it permits the formation of simultaneous images: if it does, it is perceptual; if not, it is imagistic (this point will be relevant when we come to dreams). Ordinary waking human consciousness thus has two dimensions or streams that run simultaneously—the stream of perceptual experiences and the stream of imagistic experiences—and neither excludes the other.[43] It is an important architectural fact about images and percepts, which needs to be recognized by any account of the distinction.

Having tabulated these points of difference, I now want to address four questions that arise: (a) what account to give of perception-based memory images; (b) whether images are best understood as a species of thought or concept; (c) whether the listed features necessarily belong together; and (d) what it means to describe both percepts and images as *visual*, in view of their marked differences.

(a) Memory Images

Hume was clearly motivated by the thought that images are very often derived from prior impressions and somehow owe their nature to their progenitors; hence his view that the image is a "copy" of the impression, albeit a degraded one (like a bad photocopy). The idea of a mere difference of degree is designed to accommodate this dependence. But what can we say about the dependence once we adopt the view that image and percept differ in their nature? More pointedly, how *can* there be the intimate relation between percept and image that the facts of memory suggest and yet the image differ so fundamentally from the percept? How can the image be in any sense a "revived percept"? Sartre felt this problem so strongly that he denied that memory images are really images; he couldn't reconcile his radical distinction between image and percept with the idea that the memory image is merely a "reborn percept" (as he put it). I think this is too radical a move, and I don't think we are compelled to countenance it; but the problem is real, and its solution shows something important about memory.

It should be conceded at once that the memory image cannot be merely a decayed or degraded form of the original percept; that would be to unlearn everything we have just discovered about how images differ from percepts. But I don't think we are forced to accept such a quantitative model of how memory preserves perception, as if memory worked like an inscription exposed to the eroding impacts of time and weather—as if the stored percept simply loses definition. Rather, memory is transformative, selective, and creative. Instead of the metaphor of the "reborn" or "revived" percept, we should prefer the metaphor of the "reincarnated" percept: instead of the percept lying dormant until summoned by memory, it is subject to deep transformations in its nature and relation to other psychological systems. I have no intention of trying to describe these transformations or how they are implemented; that is largely a question for empirical research. My point is rather that there is no bar in principle to our recognizing that there are such transformations. If the percept is the input to the process and the memory image is the output, then we can acknowledge that the output can differ radically from the input while also agreeing that there is a definite derivational relationship here; it is not that the image gets unmoored from the percept and can no longer be associated with it. Retinal stimulations and visual percepts are very different in nature too, and yet the latter are intelligibly derived from the former; similarly, percepts and their imagistic progeny can be intelligibly related without having to be mere versions of each other, differing only in degree. Just to give two examples of the kind of transformations I have in mind: the percept will be subject to a "de-saturation" operation that introduces the kinds of gaps I mentioned earlier; and it will be shifted to a system that can be activated by the will.[44] Both of these operations are consistent with the final image being *based on* the originating percept.

Here is a little experiment the reader might wish to try: Stare hard at some object, say, a coffee cup, then close your eyes. The percept disappears, of course, and in its place is a kind of iconic trace, the residue of the retinal stimulation that has just been curtailed; it is phenomenologically in the visual field, a kind of copy of the original percept, and it wanes extremely quickly. As soon as you can after closing your eyes, try to summon an image of the previously seen cup. I think you will find that this takes something like a second and cannot be rushed (this is not a very hi-tech experiment). What comes to mind is a very different animal from the iconic trace that has recently vanished, and it bears all the marks of images that I tabulated earlier. During this intense second, I surmise, the memory systems have carried out the transformations necessary to convert percept to image, and these are nontrivial—as the time lag would suggest. The percept has been dismantled, analyzed, reconstructed, relocated, and then made ready for imagistic recall. It has not merely languished idly while the vividness has bled out of it. The memory image is to the percept what the butterfly is to the caterpillar—the end product of metamorphosis. The two need not be assimilated in order to be recognized as close relations: derivation is not the same as reduction.

(b) Are Images Thoughts?

In distinguishing images from percepts, I often likened images to thoughts, in contrast to percepts; this may have suggested to the reader a very different assimilation from Hume's, namely that images should be identified with acts of thinking—with the exercise of concepts.[45] Certainly, if you look through my list of *differentia*, images and thoughts are strikingly similar in their properties: they are both subject to the will, not a matter of conducting observations, lacking in a visual (or other) field, not saturated, attention-dependent, often about absent objects, non-recognitional, and non-occlusive. Couple these points with the fact that images are caused by intentional states (desire and intention) and apparently thought-laden, and a reduction to thoughts starts to seem an attractive idea. Thus an image of my mother is really a congeries of thoughts, such as: my mother has blond hair, blue eyes, a freckle on her left cheek, et cetera. I bring together a series of descriptive thoughts, and their totality *is* an image of my mother. Here we have a "propositional" theory of the image: the image is a conjunction of propositions entertained simultaneously. The old empiricist theory was that concepts can be identified with sensory images; the current theory is that images can be reduced to concepts—episodes of thinking.

But I would reject such a reduction for two reasons—one obvious, the other less so. First, the concept theory cannot do justice to the sensory character of the image. There is something it is like to have a visual image, and this something is in important respects similar to what it is like to have a visual percept: both, after all, are aptly described as *visual*. Both involve simultaneous presentations of a number of visually detectable features—color, shape, and so on. The mental state I am in when I form a visual image of my mother is very different from the state I would be in if I simply entertained a number of descriptive thoughts about her; indeed, I could do the latter without being able to imaginatively represent her at all. An image is no more *reducible* to acts of thinking than a percept is. I take it that this is a familiar enough line of thought not to need elaborate statement.

The less obvious reason goes back to a remark of Wittgenstein's: "While I am looking at an object I cannot imagine it." Let me first spell out this point. The claim is not that I cannot imagine *anything* while I am looking at (better, seeing) an object; it is that I cannot imagine the very object I am looking at. Seeing X and imagining X exclude each other. This is still not precise enough, however: for I can surely be looking at Jones from the back, not even realize I am looking at Jones, and still imagine him from the front. *De re* seeing does not prevent *de dicto* imagining. What we need is this: I cannot imagine X in the very same *way* that I am currently seeing X; I cannot form an image of X that mimics the way X is currently appearing to me. In other words, I cannot simultaneously have a percept and an image whose *content* is the same: I cannot, say, be seeing a red cube at the same time as imagining one.

Now, I think Wittgenstein is right about this, and perhaps we can understand why the claim is true by consulting our list: for it is not possible to be both passive and active with respect to the same mental content, not possible to be both observational and not, not possible to represent the same thing as absent and present.[46] But whatever the reason for this particular exclusion relation between image and percept, it appears intuitively correct. And I think it has a significant bearing on any assimilation between images and concepts. Suppose we identify image I with concept C (possibly complex). Now, consider looking at something, X, which falls under C, where C gives the appearance of X: C might be *red cube*. Surely in looking at X and taking in its appearance, I can also *judge* that X is C: I can judge that the object I am seeing is a red cube. The whole point of such concepts is to be applicable to perceptually presented objects. But if Wittgenstein's point is right, I cannot form an image of something that is C, since seeing something that is C excludes that. Therefore I cannot be identical to C. I cannot form an image of a red cube while I am seeing one, but I can apply the concept *red cube* to a red cube I am seeing; so the image and the concept cannot be identical. The concept can combine with the percept, but the image cannot. Notice that this refutes both directions of reduction. It refutes the empiricist doctrine that concepts are reducible to images, because it excludes the paradigm case of applying a concept to a seen object; and it refutes the cognitivist reduction of images to concepts (and hence thoughts), because it would allow images to be formed in the perceptual presence of the seen object. So Wittgenstein's point is a powerful and sharp tool in resisting the assimilation of images and concepts. Not that he used it in this way, which is odd given his interest in the imagery theory of concepts.[47] For me, the argument just given supplies an extra reason to reject the reduction of images to descriptive thoughts: you can clearly think about an object while you are seeing it, but you cannot form an image of it.

Images are therefore neither percepts nor thoughts. One tradition seeks to reduce thoughts to percepts—the empiricists. Another seeks to reduce percepts to thoughts—the cognitivists (for want of a better term). Both of these reductions now command few adherents. Percepts and thoughts are different *kinds* of mental item, with different kinds of intentionality. Images are also often claimed to be reducible to some other kind of mental phenomenon—either to percepts or to thoughts. I have found good reasons to reject both sorts of reduction. My conclusion, then, is that images are *sui generis*, and should be added as a third great category of intentionality to the twin pillars of perception and cognition. There are *three* irreducibly different modes of intentionality to contend with. Nor would it be correct to construe images as some sort of *amalgam* of percepts and concepts—a percept with a thought accompaniment, say. For, as we have seen, images are not percepts at all, so they are not *partially* percepts. The sensory material of the image does not occur in the form of a percept. Neither is it at all obvious that images necessarily carry a thought component: might not animals and babies have mental images and yet not be capable of conceptual thought?[48] Images are not *constructs* out of percepts and thoughts; they are not combinations of the other two modes of intentionality. Rather, they are a distinctive type of mental category, which needs to be acknowledged in its own right. Images are not just minor variations on perception and thought, of negligible theoretical interest; they are a robust mental category in need of independent investigation.

(c) Are the Features Separable?

Here I simply want to raise a hard question, not provide a definitive answer. I have listed a set of features that distinguish images from percepts, but do these features *necessarily* belong together? Can we conceive of a type of mind in which, say, there are experiences that are both subject to the will and yet not attention-dependent? Can there be experiences that carry a visual field but are not accompanied by the observational attitude? Does non-occlusion necessarily go with non-recognition? These questions are connected to the question of the logical dependence of the cited features; in particular, can some of the features be derived from others (for example, subjection to the will from attention-dependence)? None of these questions is easy, and I have nothing very conclusive to say about them. I think it would be surprising if the features could be easily pulled apart, because they are not found apart as things actually are, and there are clear connections between some of them—as with subjection to the will and the non-recognitional knowledge of the object of the image. But trying to forge hard modal connections between all the features would be a large and difficult task.

The question is not entirely theoretical either. For the case of dreams might well seem like one in which some of the characteristics of images are present but not all: dreams do not seem subject to the dreamer's will, but neither do they involve any recognition of the identity of the objects dreamed about; you just *know* whom you are dreaming about. I am going to discuss this matter at length later, but I mention it now so that we can see the relevance of a rarified-sounding question. In particular, we need to ask whether images and percepts, as characterized so far, are the *only* kinds of sensory mental representation there could be: could there be a type of experience that deserved to be called *visual* and yet was neither a visual percept nor a visual image? Might dream experiences be precisely that? If we subtract some of the features of images and keep others, do we generate a new category of sensory experience—or do we have the old images shorn of a contingent characteristic? Are such questions answerable at all? Are they even meaningful?

So let us be content for now to have listed the *actual* distinguishing features of images, and leave the question of images in other possible worlds for another occasion (or life).

(d) In What Sense Are Images Visual?

For all its other defects, the Humean conception does have one signal advantage: it can neatly explain exactly why images are classified as visual, auditory, and so on. It's because they simply *are* faded percepts. And perhaps it was this question that partly encouraged Hume's oversimplified theory. For it does seem that this is a nonnegotiable fact about images—that they bear a phenomenological resemblance to percepts. The easiest way to explain this is to say that they are percepts of some sort. But what account can be given of this phenomenal similarity if we accept the view of images I have been advocating? How *can* images be visual, say, if they differ so dramatically from visual percepts? It seems as if the image lacks the very marks that make an experience *visual*. Certainly, if we regard visual percepts as the prototype—the paradigm—then we can find only a derivative sense in which images can be visual, if that. Is it only because images are generally *derived* from percepts that we by courtesy call images by sensory names? Is there nothing *intrinsically* visual about them? And yet, they do seem to bear a *phenomenal* similarity to percepts. We have a puzzle here: how are the differences between images and percepts compatible with the fact that both can be classified according to the name for a sense modality?[49] This question is closely connected to the question of the propriety of the term "the mind's eye": is this a mere metaphor, or does it have literal truth of some sort? How can the organ that generates images be likened to the organ that generates percepts? With what right do we employ the concept of an inner *eye*? These questions will be taken up in the next chapter.

The Mind's Eye

We speak of seeing in (or with) the mind's eye: but how literally should this talk of *seeing* be taken? When I visualize something, do I really see it? Or does "in the mind's eye" function to cancel the implication of seeing—as with "fake" in "fake gold"? Is seeing with "the body's eye" the only genuine kind of seeing? And if so, what becomes of the idea that visual imagery is genuinely visual? In general, what is the conceptual relationship between seeing with the body's eye and seeing with the mind's eye? Is the former more basic, so that the latter is an extended (or overextended) use? I shall argue, to the contrary, that the mind's eye does afford a kind of seeing, that the experiences it delivers are straightforwardly visual, and that the phrase "the mind's eye" is not metaphorical. It is literally true that we see with our mind; "mindsight" is not an oxymoron (unlike "blindsight").

The reasons against postulating a mind's eye are obvious: there is nothing in the brain that resembles the anatomical eyes that adorn the top half of our faces. There is no organ in the brain with a cornea, a lens, a retina, and so on that interacts with light to produce a percept. Now, I am not about to announce a startling empirical discovery to the effect that such a structure has just been discovered buried deep within the occipital cortex; the points I want to bring up are entirely conceptual. The question I am interested in is whether the so-called mind's eye involves a type of genuinely visual experience that can take external things as its intentional objects. If so, it is a type of seeing (in the relevant sense). Suppose I form an image of the Eiffel Tower: do I thereby visually apprehend the Eiffel Tower? Is that object presented to my mind in the visual mode?

In order to be clear on this, we need to be clear about the role of the body's eyes in generating visual awareness of things. And the answer is that they work as *transducers* of information; they convert light energy into neural impulses. They are *not* the basis of visual experience itself, obviously. That honor belongs to the visual cortex: *it* is the organ that makes visual experience possible. The external eye merely sends inputs into this visual organ; and it is perfectly possible to have visual experiences and have no external eyes at all. So the organ of visual experience is really the brain.[1] But of course this must also be true of visual imagery: there must be a part of the brain that is the basis of this type of experience. In *that* sense, we have an inner eye: we have an anatomical system that produces visual representations of external objects (assuming that images can be literally described as visual). We need not quibble here about the correct use of the word "eye" (i.e., how much of the body's visual system it should be taken to include); for my purposes it is enough that we agree that we have an organ that generates visual experiences when we entertain visual images. We can be said to have an inner eye if we have an organ that generates visual presentations of external objects in the process of forming mental images. The more difficult question is what justifies calling this type of experience *visual;* once this is agreed, the question of whether we have a mind's eye becomes trivially terminological.[2]

Suppose there were a species that had only visual imagery, with no visual perception. They describe their images using a concept *see**. Now, one day, by some mutation, they start to have visual percepts, which are quite new to them. They wonder how to describe these novel experiences; in particular, they wonder whether *see** applies to them. The new experiences certainly differ from the images they have had hitherto, but they are also similar in obvious ways. Some speakers begin to speak of "seeing* with the body's eye," and an issue arises as to whether this is a literally correct usage. There are those who regard the new usage as illegitimate, meta-phorical at best, a bit of poetic license; and those who are inclined not to balk at this application of *"see*,"* finding it literally correct. This species is clearly the inverse of our species. And many of them are understandably inclined to take their original use as basic and the new use as derivative, or defective. Now, I think we should be critical of this view; we should suspect them of indulging in Misplaced Conceptual Primacy. For, given our linguistic practices, we regard visual percepts as the primary type of visual experience. My suggestion is that we are *both* guilty of that sin: neither use is primary or proprietary. I want to say that there is a single notion of the visual of which both visual percepts and visual images are exemplifications; the genus *seeing* has two species, neither of which is superordinate over the other. The advantage of this view (aside from its simplicity and naturalness) is that it explains how both per-cepts and images can equally count as visual, since *neither* category is taken as paradigmatic; both are taken as variations on a single theme—what we might call "visual apprehension." This notion cannot be explained by alluding to what is distinctive of percepts or images, but must be taken to capture what is common between them.[3]

This suggestion will not recommend itself if we make the mis-take of supposing that visualizing is the same as imagining that one sees. For then the concept of perceptual seeing is built into the definition of visual imagining, and there is no symmetrical building of the concept of imagery into the definition of seeing. But it is easy to see that such a definition is wide of the mark: imagining that one sees is neither necessary nor sufficient for visualizing. Not nec-essary, because I can visualize something without imagining that I am seeing it: that would involve me in imagining myself to have a visual experience, but I need not imagine anything about *myself* in order to visualize some other object. Not sufficient, because I might imagine myself seeing something by forming an image of myself standing in front of that thing with my eyes open—but this falls short of my visualizing that thing. Visualizing the Eiffel Tower and imagining (i.e., visualizing) that I am seeing the Eiffel Tower are intentional acts with very different contents. Nor would it be correct to say that when I visualize something it is *as if* I see it—any more than to see something is *as if* one is imagining it.[4] It is not *as if* I am seeing the Eiffel Tower when I visualize it, since I have no tendency to conflate the visualizing with the seeing. If I am hallucinating the Eiffel Tower, then this is indeed as if I am seeing it; but, as we have seen, images and hallucinations are not to be assimilated, since hallucinations are simply percepts without an external object. So there is no basis here for insisting that perceptual seeing is conceptually fundamental.

Another source of potential error is to suppose that images don't "make contact" with external objects but only with some supposed mental realm (the analogue of the sense-datum theory of perception). In thinking this way, it will seem that images and percepts have quite different kinds of intentional objects. But we should hold fast to the commonsense view that images can be *of* external physical things—so they can be of exactly what percepts can be of. Of course, it is true that images can be of nonexistent things, but this is also true of percepts, as in the case of hallucination. I would advocate "naïve realism" about imagery, in the sense that physical objects are typically what we imagine. Given that, visual imagery is precisely visual experience that is directed toward physical objects, just like regular seeing. The image itself is the *vehicle* of intentionality, just as the percept is; it is certainly not the *object* of imagistic intentionality. So there is no asymmetry between seeing and visualizing here that could motivate withholding the word "see" from the case of imagery.

In my view, then, "see" is univocal in both sorts of use. We add the adverb phrase "in the mind" to distinguish one kind of seeing from the other kind (compare "thinking out loud" and "thinking silently"—both kinds of thinking). But if this is right, then it is not quite correct to say, after all, that seeing is passive and not subject to the will; for this is true of only *one* kind of seeing—the "with the body" kind. It makes sense to order someone to visualize a certain object, because this is an action that comes within the scope of the person's will; but "visualize" is just a variant of "see with the mind's eye," so it ought to make sense to order someone to see an object with her mind's eye—and I think it does. I might, for example, be doing an experiment on imagery and ask my subjects to see a rainbow with their mind's eye. This is perhaps a bit stilted, but I don't think it violates the grammar of the term. By contrast, if I were doing an experiment on ordinary visual perception and instructed my subjects to see things, that would be an exercise in futility. So *some* seeing is active; the verb "see" can express an action as well as a passion. And similarly for "hear": "Hear the opening bars of Beethoven's Fifth!" makes perfectly good sense in the context of a discussion about hearing music "in the head," though not when we are talking about using those flaps on either side of the head. It is notable here that adverbs of action can attach themselves to "see" in the imagery use, though not in the perceptual use. I might speak of guiltily seeing something in my mind's eye, but I cannot sensibly speak of guiltily seeing something with my outer eye (of course, I can guiltily *look* at something). The mind's eye, then, is an active organ: its associated visual experiences are subject to the will. Seeing can be something that you *do* (and do intentionally).[5]

I want to make one final point about the mind's eye before ending this short chapter, the chief purpose of which has been to legitimate the sensory credentials of the imaginative faculty—that is, to show how it is possible for the concept of the *visual* to apply to (certain) images. We speak of the mind's eye in the singular; we don't talk about the mind's eye*s*. We don't suppose that we have two mind's eyes, to match the two bodily eyes. Why is this? One might have thought that we would just carry over our usual ways of talking from the outer to the inner, but we seem on the contrary to presuppose a Cyclopean conception of seeing in the mind. The question is perplexing, but here are two relevant considerations. First, depth seems poorly represented in visual images; visual percepts convey a much more pronounced presentation of depth. But, as is well known, binocular disparity is one the main engines of depth perception. The lack of depth in the image might then be taken to evidence the absence of such binocular disparity. It seems conceivable that a creature should have two imagery devices in its brain that project a slight disparity in the way the represented object is presented, so that combining them will yield a better sense of depth; but that does not seem to be the case with our imagery system. It seems modestly monocular. Second, and I hope not too frivolously, we never have the experience of closing one inner eye while leaving the other open; visual imagination is all or nothing. We certainly don't have the experience of closing one inner eye and then noticing a reduction in depth perception! So here again is a little bit of a rationale for our habitual ways of talking. Of course, it may be that even asking this question—"how many mind's eyes do we have?"—is misguided, an overly slavish adherence to the model provided by the body's eyes; but if I were forced to answer the question, I would favor the verdict suggested by grammar: one. That means we have three eyes altogether.[6]

Imaginative Seeing

I have so far spoken as if images and percepts were entirely discrete, occupying hermetically sealed pockets of the mind. And, given their radically different natures, such a separation might well seem inevitable. There does exist a hybrid form, however—imaginative seeing—and we need to add this to our inventory of sensory representations. Much of what I say in this chapter will be familiar,[1] but there are some points that need to be emphasized and their significance appreciated; I also want to bring out how puzzling imaginative seeing is, in the light of the points made in Chapter 1.

In his famous discussion of "seeing as" in the *Philosophical Investigations,* Wittgenstein introduces the example of a triangle, which he reproduces on the page, and he says: "This triangle can be seen as a triangular hole, as a solid, as a geometrical drawing; as standing on its base, as hanging from its apex; as a mountain, as a wedge, as an arrow or pointer, as an overturned object that is meant to stand on the shorter side of the right angle, as a half parallelogram, and as various other things."[2] Thus the concept of seeing-as is introduced by first generating a percept in the reader and then suggesting a number of different "interpretations" that can be imaginatively placed on it. Several pages later he writes: "The aspects of the triangle: it is as if an *image* came into contact, and for a time remained in contact, with the visual impression."[3] Expanding this thought he says:

> The concept of an aspect is akin to the concept of an image. In other words: the concept "I am now seeing it as . . ." is akin to "I am now having *this* image."
>
> Doesn't it take imagination to hear something as a variation on a particular theme? And yet one is perceiving something in so hearing it.
>
> "Imagine this changed like this, and you have this other thing." One can use imagination in the course of proving something.
>
> Seeing an aspect and imagining are subject to the will. There is such an order as "Imagine *this*," and also: "Now see the figure like *this*"; but not: "Now see this leaf green."[4]

Clearly, these passages accord nicely with the passages I quoted in Chapter 1 from *Zettel*, where Wittgenstein also speaks of the image as being "subject to the will." His thought, then, is that the seeing of aspects is imaginative and therefore inherits the voluntariness of imagining, and yet it is a kind of seeing; while non-imaginative seeing (like seeing the green leaf) is not subject to the will. We might say that the perceptual component of a case of seeing-as (such as seeing the triangle) is not subject to the will, but the imaginative component is; yet the two fuse in a special kind of visual experience that is neither simple percept nor simple image. Rather, it is as if the image comes to permeate the percept, to inhabit it, reach out to it, clothe it—the metaphors come easily here (perhaps too easily). The puzzle is how such a fusion of contraries is possible, given that it is a fact of experience.[5]

Let us first round out the notion of imaginative seeing. I would distinguish three broad categories of imaginative seeing: the seeing of aspects, the seeing of pictures, and imagination-driven perceptual distortions.[6] The first of these was Wittgenstein's chief concern: the duck/rabbit case is the most familiar. Here we can see the object (lines on paper) in one way or the other; the figure is "ambiguous"—open to multiple interpretation. The second includes the seeing of pictorial representations as picturing some object or state of affairs. We may have a simple percept of the picture, with no imagination involved, and then we have the consciousness of what it represents—and this requires an exercise of imagination. Sometimes it takes awhile before the representative character of the picture becomes evident; but when it does, the imagination comes into play, and we may not be able to see it as anything *other* than a representation of X. As with seeing aspects, this kind of seeing involves a move away from the simple percept, though the percept is what makes this transcendence possible: the imaginative seeing is *based on* the percept, triggered by it. The third category includes such cases as seeing branches at night as the limbs of fearsome monsters, or a stranger in the street as someone one used to know well. These are typically affect-driven—by fear or desire—and they generally involve seeing something as other than it is. It may be that the present percept simply elicits a memory image, which thereupon attaches itself to the percept of the moment. In all three categories we have a percept being invaded by an act of imagination: instead of the image remaining in its own "space," a representation of an absent object, it locates its object within the current visual field.[7] Compare forming an image of a duck and seeing lines on paper *as* a duck: the duck image seems to have made a trip from imaginative space to real perceived space. Suppose I am having images of X and then I see a stranger on the street who strongly resembles X. I might well see that stranger *as* X, and now my image has made the leap to perceptual space. As Wittgenstein remarks, evidently with a sense of perplexity (which I share), it is as if the image and the percept have come into contact. The resulting sensory experience is a joint product of the outer eyes and the inner eye—a strange coalescence of opposites.

Thus imaginative seeing is subject to the will, in virtue of its image component—though not, of course, "all the way down," since I cannot alter the core percept at will. But what about the other features I listed in Chapter 1? The seeing-as experience will include both an observational and a non-observational attitude on the part of the perceiver: I am open to the informational opportunities provided by the perceived object, but I do not expect to learn more about the aspect I bring it under—for that is supplied by me. I do not gaze at the duck aspect in hopes of learning more about ducks, though the duck/rabbit drawing may engage my curiosity; just as I do not gain information about the person depicted in a portrait just by imagining him, though I may learn a lot about painting by staring at the canvas and taking in what it offers to my senses. The object of my perception is observed by me, but the object of my imagining is not; nothing new comes to me from the image itself, since it is constituted by what I bring to it.[8] Seeing as thus brings with it a mixture of the observational attitude and its lack.

What about indeterminacy? Suppose I see a feather duster as a speckled hen. The resulting experience may well leave it indeterminate how many speckles my imagined hen has; there will be gaps in the sensory representation, areas of unsaturatedness. The projected aspect will exhibit the kind of "poverty" I discussed earlier. And yet my percept of the duster itself will be as filled in as any percept. So, again, we find percept and image incongruously (though naturally!) combined, displaying both sensory saturation and the lack of it.

Attention-dependence? My attention can wander from the object of my percept without sacrificing the percept, but can it wander from the aspect I am imaginatively seeing and the aspect remain? I think not. If my attention is distracted from the duck/rabbit drawing, it can still stay within my visual field and be seen by me; but I cannot, so distracted, persist in seeing it under any aspect. The figure degenerates into a mere pattern of lines. Suppose I form an image of the Eiffel Tower as my eyes are confronted by the duck/rabbit drawing—which is perfectly possible. I cannot then *also* see it *as* a duck (or a rabbit). The aspect requires my attention for it to be visually available; it belongs to the category of "attentive intentionality." This is also why it is so hard to have imaginative sensings from different senses simultaneously: I cannot see X as Y at the same time as hearing Z as W (without a division of attention), where these are both cases of imaginative sensing. And what sense does it make to say that the absentminded truck driver sees imaginatively as his mind wanders? If he suddenly sees a moving car as a rogue elephant, he *necessarily* focuses his attention on what he is seeing; he cannot see *as* while his attention is focused on his forthcoming dinner—though he can see *simpliciter*. Seeing-as competes with the concurrent image, unlike plain seeing.[9]

The question of absence and the visual field is subtle. Is the duck aspect seen as *in* my visual field when I see the duck/rabbit drawing that way? Is the person depicted seen as *before* me when I look at his portrait? The answer appears to be affirmative in that the infused percept represents a present object. But on more careful thought that sounds oversimplified: Do I really believe there is a drawing of a duck in front of me? Do I actually think I am standing in front of Winston Churchill? No: I believe that there is an ambiguous figure there, and a portrait of Churchill. I do not literally locate the imagined objects in my visual field; they are not there for me in the same way the lines and canvas are. Perhaps I can be fooled into thinking they are there, in cases like seeing the branches as limbs. But once I know that I am only imagining this, I do not suppose that I am seeing any limbs; the limbs retreat to my imagination. What I am seeing in my visual field is merely similar to limbs. The aspect is not then presented as present in the fullest sense; we might say that it is merely *as if* it is present—a kind of sensory pretense. It is not present in the way the object of my percept is present.[10]

Can I misidentify an imagined aspect? Suppose I misidentify some lines on a page as a duck/rabbit drawing and have the corresponding percept (so that I am under a perceptual illusion); then I start to see the illusory object *as* a rabbit (compare seeing the lines in the Muller-Lyer illusion as a pair of train rails of unequal length). Can I also misidentify what I am seeing it *as*, so that I am really seeing it as a duck but it seems to me that I am seeing it as a rabbit? I think not. My percept misidentifies the original drawing, but my imagination does not misidentify the aspect under which it brings this drawing: I know for sure that I am seeing it as a rabbit, because this interpretation comes from me.[11] So, once again, we have a mixture of percept and image with the predictable combination of features: the core percept allows for misidentification, but the superimposed aspect does not; my senses can fool me, but my imagination cannot (at least in this particular respect).

Finally, occlusion: is the aspect occlusive? Clearly not. When I start to see the duck/rabbit drawing as a duck, I do not stop seeing the lines I saw before; there is no blocking of my visual field by the aspect. The aspect adds to what I see, it does not subtract from it. This is very different from being under the illusion that a red object is green; in that case I am not also seeing the object as red. Here the percepts compete. But there is no such competition between seeing the canvas and seeing it *as* a portrait of X. The visible features of an object are not occluded by imaginatively seeing it a certain way; they are merely supplemented. The imagined aspect does compete with other acts of imagination, as I noted earlier, but it does not compete with the core percept; indeed, the core percept is the *sine qua non* of imaginative seeing-as.

So the phenomenon of imaginative seeing should not cause us to revise what I said earlier about images and percepts, though we do need to introduce some extra subtlety and complexity into the picture.

Not all seeing is seeing-as, as Wittgenstein intends the notion. Of course, in ordinary speech it is not wrong to use the locution "seeing as" in a more liberal manner: I might speak of seeing the apple as green or the building as cubical. But imaginative seeing is a different matter; as Wittgenstein remarks, it makes no sense to order someone to see something as green. Objects are seen as having various properties, but these "aspects" are not subject to the will and do not count as imaginative seeing. Nor do they prevent the formation of simultaneous images: I can see the apple as green and form an image of something else at the same time; so the seeing I am engaged in is not recruiting the imagination—which is why I can deploy my imagination elsewhere. Most seeing is of this non-imaginative kind, or else we could not enjoy a simultaneous stream of mental images. The intentionality of perception is not then derived from the intentionality of imagination, as Hume seems to have thought; the role of imagination in perception is limited.[12]

It would also be wrong to take hallucination and illusion as *eo ipso* imaginative seeing. Hallucinations and illusions are no more subject to the will than veridical perception; you cannot stop seeing the lines in the Muller-Lyer illusion as unequal just by trying to. The causation of these perceptual states does not go via the will. The perpetually hallucinating brain in a vat is not controlling its sensory experience in the way characteristic of imagery. In these cases there is no use of the mind's eye; the systems deployed are those that serve the body's eye—though now detached from the eye's normal input. There is as much of a visual field in hallucinatory cases as in veridical cases, and our attitude is equally observational. Not surprisingly, then, it is possible to form images while hallucinating or being under a sensory illusion, since these states do not call upon imaginative resources. If a person's cortex is being electrically stimulated by a surgeon in just the way that it is in the ordinary case, there is no block to forming images at the same time. The brain in a vat can entertain images as well as you or I. So hallucinations cannot themselves be images. Moreover, hallucination and illusion are rightly classified as malfunctions: the visual system is not behaving as it is supposed to. But forming an image of something that isn't there is *not* a malfunction; so the two concepts are quite different. The only way that hallucination resembles imagery is that in both cases the intentional object is not required to exist; but this is not universally true, since many images are of existent things, and anyway does not make hallucinations resemble images in all the other ways I have discussed.

It is worth noting, however, that, although hallucinations are not generally images, they *can* involve imaginative seeing, at least in principle. If I hallucinate a duck/rabbit drawing and then see it as a rabbit, then I *am* engaging in imaginative seeing, except that I am hallucinating, not seeing (veridically). Percepts and images can make contact even when the percept is non-veridical ("hallucinating as"). So there may be aspects of human psychology that fall under this heading, in which case some hallucinations do involve the imagination, just as some veridical percepts do. It is certainly worth considering whether dreams, say, are of this mental type, or the delusions of the psychotic—that is, hallucinatory core percepts suffused with imaginative content. To our simple taxonomy of images and percepts, then, we need to add the categories of imaginative seeing and imaginative hallucinating. But these hybrids do not alter the fundamental picture sketched in Chapter 1: there is still a deep divide between the percept and the image.

The Space of Imagery

In visual perception space is represented, but is space represented in visual imagery—and if so, is it the same space? Imagery seems anomalously related to space; it seems to be somehow both spatial and non-spatial. How exactly is space represented in imagery, if it is? In considering these questions I again take my cue from Wittgenstein:

> One would like to say: The imaged is in a different *space* from the heard sound.
>
> (Question: Why?) The seen in a different space from the imaged.
>
> Hearing is connected with listening; forming an image of a sound is not.
>
> That is why the heard sound is in a different space from the imagined sound.[1]

A little later he reiterates this thought: "What is imaged is not in the same *space* as what is seen. Seeing is connected with looking."[2] Now, I do not for a moment pretend that any of this is very clear, but I do think that Wittgenstein is tapping into an intuition here that deserves articulation; so let us see how far we can get in making sense of all this.

To begin with, the point is not that the image itself is in a different space from the percept; it is that the *object* of the image is in a different space from the object of the percept. To be more exact, the object is *located* in a different space by these two mental acts. Nor is this the trivial thought that the imaged object is represented as located in another *part* of (ordinary) space. No, the thought appears to be that imagery brings with it another *kind* of space altogether. The space of perception and the space of imagery are different, and presumably not unified in any way. This makes the case different from, say, the space of vision and the space of touch. Here it would be implausible to say that these two senses are directed at different spaces (though the view has been maintained, especially by sense-datum theorists); what we have is the same space presented in two different ways, visually or tactually. And these two ways of presenting space are unified in such a way that we do not ordinarily think that we are confronted by two kinds of space. But the case of imagery seems different: here talk of two incommensurable spaces sounds much more intuitive, if highly obscure and problematic. What can it *mean*?

Wittgenstein's own response to this problematic idea is deflationary. He seems to be saying that the intuition in question amounts to no more than the fact that in seeing we look and in hearing we listen, but that we do not do these things when we imagine. It is hard to know exactly what he has in mind here, given the brevity of his comments, but the thought seems to be that looking and listening are space-directed actions, but nothing comparably space-directed goes on with imagery. Because of these spatially directed actions in the case of perception, we treat the two spaces as different. But this seems to be a way of saying that the initial intuition is an illusion: there aren't really two spaces in seeing and visualizing; it's just that we misconstrue the connection to looking as if it introduced another space. But why should this agreed connection give rise to such an outlandish idea? And if there were no such connection, would we have no tendency to speak of two spaces? If a creature could see but not look, would it have no inclination to posit a distinct space for visual imagery? I think the intuition springs from the intrinsic phenomenology of percepts and images, not from their differential relation to the act of looking.[3] So I cannot make much of Wittgenstein's deflationary explanation.

I suggest we try another explanation. First, let us remind ourselves that images are neutral as to the actual spatial relations of their objects. If I form an image of my friend Peter, I do not represent him as in any definite spatial relation to me or to other objects, whereas if I see Peter, he must be spatially located by my perceptual experience. Thus imagery is *non-locating,* unlike perception. Still, this doesn't settle the question of whether Peter is represented as himself occupying a particular region of space, despite the lack of specificity about his spatial relations. Do I represent the region of space he is in when I imagine him? Here we need to compare imagery with perception, on the one hand, and thought, on the other. If I see Peter, I thereby see or visually represent the space he occupies: that region of space falls within my visual field and I am aware of it. As he moves through space, I visually represent the successive regions of space he occupies. In the perception of objects, perception of space comes with the territory; it is automatic, built in. But in the case of thought, none of this is so: if I think of Peter, without perceiving him, I do not thereby think of the space he occupies. Conceptual intentionality is more discriminating than that; it can, so to speak, peel Peter off from the space he occupies. This is why I can think of him and have no information whatsoever about his spatial location (this cannot be so when I perceive him, since he is presented in perceiver-centered space). The concept can be much more *selective* than the percept. So there *is* no space of thought— no representation of space that necessarily goes with thinking of objects. Thoughts do not represent objects as within a spatial manifold in the way percepts do (though they might in other ways).[4]

But what should we say about images? They fall midway between percepts and thoughts. They are sensory and admit the notion of expanse: the imagined object is represented as extended.

But they do not present the object as located in space in the way percepts do. They are selective in the way concepts are, but they are not intrinsically non-spatial. Thus I do not represent the space Peter is in when I form an image of him, yet he is presented to me as a spatial being—as extended and dimensional.[5] I suggest that it is this ambiguous status of the image—that it is suspended between percept and concept—that accounts for the odd way that we take images to relate to space. We are tempted by the idea of a distinct space because we do not represent the object as located in the space of perception, and yet the object is represented as a spatial entity. It is not that we represent the object as *not* in ordinary space but as in some other space. Rather, we fail to represent the object as in ordinary space; we do not bring that further system of representation into the picture. The image has the spatiality of all sensory representation, but it does not contain within itself a specification of spatial location, unlike ordinary perception.[6] This makes us reach for the idea of a distinct space.

No doubt this is still rather obscure—and I find it hard to make it any clearer—but it seems to correspond to something about how space and imagery connect and fail to connect. Note that it is not the idea that the image itself belongs to some mental space, different from the space out there—for that would be equally true of the percept. As I said earlier, it is the *object* of the image that we are talking about and the space it is represented as occupying. On this interpretation, then, it is not correct to say outright that the objects actually occupy distinct spaces; rather, we can come to see why such a hyperbolic statement might be prompted by genuine features of the image without being literally true (in this respect I am as deflationary as Wittgenstein).

But the matter does not quite end there, because there is another question that needs to be addressed: the question of the *frame* of the image.[7] When you form an image of something, it appears to come with a kind of border; it seems to be enclosed in a surrounding frame. This frame has a spatial character, which is why it can be said to surround and enclose the image. And this frame is mentally represented in some way: it is not represented as *part* of the image, or what the image itself is of; but it is nevertheless somehow an intentional object of an accompanying mental act. I represent the Eiffel Tower in my image *and* I represent the frame that surrounds this image. Granted that this is so (and again the matter is elusive and obscure), it raises the question of what kind of space is being represented—not the space *in* the image but the space *of* the image. We might say that this space is the *medium* of the image, not its object. Is this a purely intentional space, so that nothing existent corresponds to the intentional act in question? If not, what kind of real space might it be? It certainly does not seem as if it is ordinary physical space that is represented. The case is not at all like imagining an object to be in the room I am seeing, where the object is imagined to be in the space revealed by perception. In the case of pure imagery, there is a sensation of the object imagined being suspended in a kind of spatial limbo, exhibited in a curious kind of quasi-space. This does seem different in kind from the space of perception. I wish I could say something more illuminating about it, but the matter is so hard to pin down, introspectively and conceptually, that I will have to leave it at that. At any rate, I hope at least to have identified a phenomenon of imagery that has been systematically neglected and that forms part of its essence. This chapter will have done its job if it creates the same sense of perplexity about this phenomenon in the reader that the writer himself feels.[8]

The Picture Theory of Images

There seems to be a powerful attraction in the idea that a visual image is a mental picture.[1] When I form an image of X, it is thought, I form a mental picture of X, which is then the "immediate object" of my imaginative consciousness. This inner picture represents X, so that I am mediately conscious of X, but it is the picture itself that I most directly see with my mind's eye. Just as I may look at a photograph or television screen with my body's eye and be said to see the individuals represented there, albeit indirectly, so I may look with my mind's eye at an internal mental picture and be said to see the pictured individual, albeit indirectly. I directly see (with my mind's eye) an internal picture of the Eiffel Tower, and I indirectly see (with my mind's eye) the Eiffel Tower. Imagistic consciousness is thus held to be structurally analogous to the consciousness we have of external pictures: there is a kind of double intentionality involved, in which both the picture and what it represents become intentional objects. Images are simply *inner* pictures, arrayed before the mind's eye.

The motivation for such a view has not always been made clear, but I suspect that it is felt that the object itself is "absent" and so not available for direct apprehension. In the case of perception, the object is at least before the perceiver's eyes and hence a candidate for being an unmediated intentional object. The bodily eye can be trained upon this object. It is *present*. But when the object is absent, how is it possible for the inner eye to get it in its sights? How can I *directly* apprehend the Eiffel Tower if it is three thousand miles away and causally isolated from my present consciousness? How can my inner eye surmount this distance and the obstacles that lie between subject and object? What if I am imagining a past object that no longer exists? How can this be directly apprehended in my imaginative acts? I cannot touch an absent object, so how is it possible for me to make mental contact with one? And yet we do say that I may have an image of the Eiffel Tower or a recently demolished house. The picture theory steps in to resolve this apparent paradox: what is seen by my inner eye *is* present to me— very present indeed. It is an item that exists in my mind, literally. What could be more present and available for mental inspection than an internal picture? This picture then *represents* the absent object, which thereby becomes the indirect object of my imaginative act. Moreover, the picture resembles the object, and hence fosters the illusion that the external object is what I directly see in my mind's eye. But in fact it is the mental picture that I directly apprehend, and the absent object comes in derivatively. In this way the picture theory resolves the problem of how an absent object can be seen by the mind's eye—it happens in virtue of the existence of a distinct *present* object, the mental picture. If someone were to suggest that in ordinary perception we see what is not present, what no longer exists, what is not sending light into our eyes, what is hidden behind obstacles, we would be incredulous indeed. But if we found that this is really the way we talk, then again a picture theory of perception might seem indicated: what we directly see are present inner pictures of remote objects (items like sense-data). It is just that in the case of perception we don't have anything like this to explain, since the perceived objects are fully and sufficiently present. In the image case, however, the objects seem too cut off to be unmediated objects of sight of any kind; their changes don't even register on the image, since they are causally removed. But internal pictures are right before our mental nose, so to speak, ideally suited to be immediate intentional objects. I think, then, that the picture theory is motivated (at least in part) by what we might call the "absence problem."

In this chapter, however, I shall be arguing against the picture theory. There are a number of objections to it, which are dotted throughout the history of the subject; for the most part, then, I will be rehearsing familiar points. To begin with, there is the "medium objection": if an image is a picture, then it ought to be constructed of certain materials—the medium of representation—just as a painting is made of pigments on a canvas.[2] These materials will give the picture certain intrinsic non-intentional properties, which can themselves be objects of attention and scrutiny. I can gaze at the paints on the canvas independently of what they represent, so that there is more to the painting than what it is *of*. But in the case of the alleged mental picture there is no analogue of this: I cannot turn my attention to the materials of the image independently of what it is an image of. My awareness is confined to the intentional properties of the image; I do not see the putative medium properties with my mind's eye. This is why I cannot have the experience of first being aware of the medium properties of the image and only subsequently come to see that they represent something—as I can initially see a painting merely as a splash of color and then come to see that it depicts a sunset. There is no logical gap for the image between its materials and its intentionality; if the intentionality is subtracted, the image evaporates. But if there are no such intrinsic properties, then I cannot be said to see a picture in my mind's eye, since it is *constitutive* of being a picture that there be this partition into intentional and non-intentional properties.

A connected point is that the notion of optimal viewing conditions has no application in the case of images.[3] If I am looking at a picture, the viewing conditions will be more or less optimal: not enough light, too much light, dust in the air, someone's head in the way. But when I have an image, nothing like this seems to hold;

there are no circumstances that affect my ability to get a clear view of my alleged internal picture. Of course, I may find it more or less difficult to form an image, but what does not happen is that the image is formed and I have difficulty seeing it properly; there is no mental analogue of turning up the light on a dimly lit inner picture. But then how can it be true that imagining is *viewing* an internal picture? I no more view my images than I view my concepts, or indeed my percepts. The previous point was that there is no picture-like entity to view; the present point is that the idea of *viewing* makes no sense here. The seemingly perspicuous model of looking at an external picture with the body's eye turns out not to apply at crucial points. We are left with a mere vague metaphor where we were promised a theory.[4]

Furthermore, if the mind's eye sees an internal picture, then there must be an episode of seeing that occurs when the picture is viewed. And this episode of seeing must be a case of seeing with the mind's eye. But seeing with the mind's eye is precisely a case of imaging. So there must be a process of forming an image of the internal picture; that is, there must be an image of an image. For the initial image was said to be a picture seen with the mind's eye, and seeing something with the mind's eye is forming an image of that thing. So whenever there is an image in the mind, there must be a second image whose intentional object is the first image. But that second image is itself a picture seen with the mind's eye, so it too requires an image of *it*. And now it is obvious that we are surfing an infinite regress: for every image in the mind, there must be a distinct image of it. Aside from the fact that this is too many images for the mind to contain, the process of forming an image could never get started if such a regress were contemplated.[5] No, the simple fact is that an image does not require another image in order for it to exist; we have one image at a time, and that is quite enough.

Now, these strike me as powerful arguments, and they encourage the idea that the image is not a picture that we inwardly see but is itself a seeing (with the mind's eye) of an external object. A percept is a seeing of an external object rather than a thing seen; an image is a seeing (with the mind's eye) of an external object rather than a thing seen. But before we can accept and explore this simple view, we need to examine some further alleged reasons for adopting the picture theory of the image—reasons deriving from cognitive science. These reasons are by now very well known, so I shall not belabor them.[6] Suppose we ask subjects how many windows there are in their living room, and we instruct them to use mental images to answer. We find that the more windows there are, the longer it takes for the subjects to answer. Suppose we instruct subjects to memorize a map, and then we ask them questions about the relative locations of things on the map. We find that the greater the distance between things, the longer it takes them to answer. Suppose that we tell subjects to perform "mental rotations" of displayed figures in order to determine which figures (viewed from one angle) are identical to which (viewed from another angle). We find that the larger the rotation involved, the longer it takes them to answer. These data, and many others to the same end, seem robust; and they suggest that subjects perform mental tasks that are sensitive to the magnitudes represented in the image. They do not store the relevant information in the form of a verbal list but somehow mentally scan suitable entities. Now, what theory might be given of the nature of the mental operations performed?

Suppose for a moment that images are inner pictures that mirror the external objects that are imaged—rooms, maps, figures. If you give me a photograph of my living room and ask me to say how many windows it contains, then I will no doubt answer in such a way as to reflect the configuration of the photograph: I will look at the picture, count the windows represented on it, and then respond. Instead of counting the windows themselves, while standing in the room, I will count their representational counterparts in the photograph; and just as the former task will vary with the number of actual windows, so the latter task will vary with the number of represented windows. In the same way, if the image is an inner picture, then I will inspect its properties and answer in a way that mirrors what I *would* answer if I were inspecting the real objects. Since the image-picture is isomorphic with the external object, my "response times" will be a function of the actual spatial layout of the external object. What I could accomplish by perceiving the object in its presence I accomplish by "scanning" its internal pictorial counterpart by means of inner vision. The pictorial character of the image thus explains the experimental data.

I think I have just given a fair and accurate summary of recent work on images in cognitive science (shorn of much distracting technicality).[7] The general theme is that the picture theory predicts the experimental data: postulating inner pictures as items that are inspected and scanned predicts the correlations between response times and the properties of the things imagined. Why does it take longer to respond the more windows there are in the room? Because the inner picture of the room has more window representations in it, and these take longer to count the more of them there are. Now, this certainly seems neat and natural, as well as scientifically interesting, and it manifestly carries a commitment to the picture theory of images. And yet didn't we see earlier that the picture theory is in big trouble? How can a scientifically credentialed theory encounter such seemingly damning conceptual problems? Is there a way out? I don't think there is any way out that involves rejecting the empirical data, since these are solid enough; nor do I doubt that mental operations involving sensory images are involved in these studies—as opposed to the accessing of verbally stored information.[8] What I think has gone wrong is the neglect of an alternative account of the data—and this neglect stems from undue anxiety about the absence problem. Let me explain.

The hard fact about the experimental data is that there is a correlation between properties of the object—number of windows in the room, distance between points on the map, angular displacement—and response times. The inner picture is then brought in to explain this correlation, by dint of its isomorphism with the object.

But what is to stop us from taking the data at face value and interpreting them accordingly? Thus when the subject is asked about the number of windows in the room, he mentally inspects *the room itself*, as he does for the map and the figures: what he "scans" is not the *image* of the object but the *object*. Of course, he does this by *having* an image of the object, but the mental operations are directed not *at* the image but at its object. The intentional object of such mental operations as scanning, rotating, and inspecting is the external thing, not the image of it. Compare the mental operation of scanning a room by means of ordinary perception: I am asked how many windows are in my living room, so I go next door and have a look, scanning my eyes over the room. Obviously, here, the intentional object of the scanning operation is an external physical thing—*not* the percepts I have *in* scanning the room. I don't scan the *percepts* at all; indeed, it is hard to know what this would be. The percepts are *vehicles* of the scan, not its objects. So *what* is scanned is identical to what is seen. Now, I think the same should be said of the kind of mental scanning involved in these imagery experiments: subjects scan the *room* with their mind's eye, not their image of the room. They no more scan the image than the perceiver of the room scans his percepts. Thus the object of the scanning operation is identical to the object of the image: the room itself.[9]

The first thing to say about this alternative theory is that it predicts the data: clearly, if the subjects are scanning the external object, then their response times will be a function of the properties of the object—particularly its spatial properties. So the picture theory enjoys no advantage here; indeed, it incorporates exactly the same prediction, via the isomorphic image. Clearly, too, we get a very strong analogy with the perceptual case, since both involve the mental scanning of external objects—which is partly what the picture theorists wish to insist upon.[10] But the two theories are totally distinct, invoking quite different mechanisms and structures; in particular, there is no mental picture invoked in my alternative theory. So why not accept my alternative theory and avoid the problems with inner pictures? I can think of two reasons that might deter someone from accepting this theory (call it the "naïve theory"), neither of which is sound. These reasons lurk behind the rush to accept the picture theory, and can make the naïve theory look like a total nonstarter.

The first reason is tacit adherence to a sense-datum conception of imagining. It is assumed that we cannot be in direct mental contact with an external object but must rather be confronted by an inner item of some sort. All the motivations that have encouraged a sense-datum view of perception are carried over to the case of imagery: for example, the argument from illusion, starting from the premise that two images could be exactly alike and yet one be of a real thing and the other of an unreal thing. I have no intention here of evaluating this old (senile?) argument, or the perceptual sense-datum theory that results from it. Suffice it to say that I (along with almost everyone else) reject that theory in the case of perception, and I see no reason to limit my rejection to the case of perception. In the case of images I would say, boringly enough, that they are experiences in the having of which we apprehend external objects—though, of course, the mode of consciousness involved is imagistic, not perceptual. We must not confuse the *act* of imagining with the *object* of imagining—a fallacy seemingly more easily made in the case of images than in the case of the perception. If we tacitly accept a sense-datum conception of the image, then of course we will suppose that operations like scanning are applied to the image itself (the "image-datum")—and then the experimental data will suggest the picture view as a way to explain the correlations. The way out of this is to accept the robust outer-directedness of the image: the intentional objects of images are external objects (existent and nonexistent), not inner mental items.[11]

The second source of deterrence is, I believe, the problem of absence. How can it be true that I am (literally) scanning an absent object? How can my mind scan what isn't there? I can scan the room in front of me with my eyes, but how can I scan a room that is not present to me? How does my inner eye fix itself on an absent room and survey its contents? First, I want to note how steadfastly we speak precisely as if we can scan absent objects in our minds. We speak of mentally scanning objects when we say such things as "I counted the number of windows in my living room in my mind's eye" and "Let me envisage what the chair would look like in that corner" and "It's as far to Los Angeles as it is to London from New York" (said while holding an image of a map in mind). All these statements are about external objects and the mental processes directed toward them, not about any supposed inner pictures. When we count the number of windows "in the image," we are counting not representations but their intentional objects, that is, windows. Here as elsewhere, we must beware of use/mention confusions— of confusing the representation with the represented. Just as we speak of scanning the room with the body's eye, so we speak of scanning the room with the mind's eye; it is not that we scan something *distinct* from what we mentally see, namely, the image itself—as the picture theory claims. We say "Count the *windows*" (by means of imagery) not "Count the number of window *representations* in your image picture." What the image is *of* is the target of our mental scans, and the image is not of itself.

This naïve realist way of speaking of imagery clearly assumes that mental operations like counting and scanning can relate the mind to an absent object. That may still appear spooky: how can I *scan* something that is not present to me? I would make two points about this worry. First, consider *referring:* I can obviously refer to things that are absent; indeed, that is the whole point of reference. Referring is an intentional relation that can reach out to absent objects—so why can't scanning and counting be intentional relations that have a similarly long reach? The reason, it might be said, is that scanning is what perceptual faculties permit, and these require presence. But why should we carry *this* feature over to the case of mental scanning? Why should we insist that the two types of scanning have this in common? Why not say that imagistic scanning is characterized precisely by the fact that it can relate us to absent objects? To be sure, the scanning does not involve the reception of a stream of new information from the object, and so is not mediated by this kind of causal channel. But whoever said that it had to? Is it thereby "nonphysical" in any spooky and objectionable sense? No more than regular reference. There will be brain operations underlying imagistic scanning and possibly a history of causal contacts with the scanned absent object: aren't these enough? The mistake here is to insist that imagistic scanning be *assimilated* to perceptual scanning, that only the perceptual type of scanning really deserves the name. But this looks like another case of Misplaced Conceptual Priority. My images can take absent objects as their target, and when they do, I can mentally survey those objects: that is the simple truth of the matter.[12] In the case of the absent room, say, my inner eye successively directs itself at the several windows contained therein, casting its far-reaching gaze over the room's extent. Presumably this will involve a series of distinct images, as a result of which I will be able to supply the correct number. At no point does my attention turn to the image itself—any more than I attend to my percepts when I am counting windows with my regular eyes.

Yet there remains a puzzling question: Why exactly are the experimental data as they are? Why do response times vary with (say) the actual spatial distance over the object? It is easy to explain this for the case of perceptual scanning: the movements of the head and eyes that accompany the scanning operation match the actual distances on the perceived object or scene; roughly, it takes longer to move one's head the greater the distance one needs to survey. But this explanation does not carry over to the inner eye, since there is no such movement involved in the scanning it performs: the inner eye does not physically shift its point of focus over the object as it moves through space. Why then does greater distance on the object correlate with longer response time? Let me offer two speculations. The first is that spatial distance corresponds to computational complexity; there is simply more processing involved when the scan is over larger regions of the object, since more mental activity is required.[13] Partly this must be true in the perceptual case too: some of the response time is taken up with computational processing and not merely with head and eye movement—and the more extensive the scan, the more of this there is. Second, I think we would expect that the dynamics of the inner eye will mirror those of the outer eye: both are visual, after all, despite their deep differences, and the processing employed in the one is likely to be mirrored by the processing involved in the other.[14]

I think, then, that the empirical results on imagery do not establish the picture theory, and that another theory can accommodate them. This is all to the good, because the picture theory seems to have serious conceptual problems. My view is that we no more see pictures in our head when we have images than we see pictures in our head when we perceive; so the *structure* of the two kinds of mental act is the same—a type of direct consciousness of external objects (existent and nonexistent). The intentionality is all outer-directed in both cases. It is not that I side with those who think images are "propositional" or analogous to beliefs; rather, I deny that there is any intentional act involved that takes a mental picture as its object. I am prepared to accept that both images and percepts may have analogue characteristics; what I reject is the idea that imaging is like looking at a picture (and similarly for perceiving). There are no special objects of imagistic intentionality, distinct from the ordinary objects we perceive and think about; the "world of the imagination" is just the world we regularly inhabit (with its nonexistent unicorns and all the rest). It is not that in imagination we direct our minds to another ontological realm—those supposed internal pictures. In short, when I form an image of the Eiffel

Tower, it is the *Eiffel Tower* that is my sole intentional object—not any supposed internal replica of it, festering in the souvenir shop of my imagination.

I have saved one objection to the picture theory till last. It links with what I said in Chapter 3 about imaginative seeing. According to the picture theory, to form an image of X is to see with the mind's eye a picture of X. Now, the seeing of pictures *as* pictures— that is, as having representational properties—is a kind of imaginative seeing. So the seeing of a mental picture as, say, a picture of the Eiffel Tower—which is required for having an image of the Eiffel Tower—will be a case of imaginative seeing, and hence will recruit the imaginative faculty. It will involve connecting an image with a percept. So the requisite type of seeing will already involve an exercise of imagination. How then can it be used to give a *theory* of the imagination? The picture theory does not *explain* imagination; it *presupposes* it.[15] If we now ask what is involved in this imaginative act—the act of seeing the internal picture as a picture of X—then we cannot answer that it also is a case of seeing a mental picture, for then we are obviously surfing a regress again. We can never see one picture without already seeing another. So the picture theory is viciously regressive. Since it must invoke a mental act of seeing-as— seeing-as with the mind's eye—it must presuppose an act of imagination, and it cannot go on to explain this by using the idea of the inner picture, on pain of regress. Only if the internal seeing were not imaginative seeing could this regress be avoided, but this is incompatible with the fact that seeing pictures as pictures is *not* the ordinary kind of seeing. And of course there is no such objection to the naïve theory, since it does not posit any seeing of pictures as at the heart of imagery.

So is there nothing to be said for the picture theory at all? Not quite: what images share with pictures is the simultaneous representation of an ensemble of properties—as well as an association with a particular sense-modality. Pictures are visual and composite, and so are images (the visual kind). This seems enough to warrant our occasional use of the word "picture" in connection with images, as in "Picture your mother's face in your mind's eye!" But this modest similarity should not be inflated into the claim that images are just one type of picture, the mental kind, which we see inwardly. The analogy should not be pressed too far.[16]

What Are Dreams?

It appears evident that during sleep we have experiences of specific sensory types. These experiences have the mark of a sense-modality upon them: they are visual or auditory or tactile et cetera. That is, there is a *similarity* between these experiences and others which characteristically occur during waking life, and which carry sensory identities. They are similar to both percepts and images; thus a given dream experience may strike us as phenomenally similar to visual percepts and visual images. The three types of experience form a phenomenal family—a likeness in what it is like. Yet there are clear differences between the members of this family; the family resemblance comes in three broad varieties. So far I have drawn a sharp distinction between the image and the percept, but have postponed the question of where dreams fall. The question I want to explore now is whether dreams belong to the image category or the percept category. Is it the mind's eye that is active during sleep or the body's eye (closed as it is)? Is it the imaginative faculties that are employed to generate dream experiences or is it the perceptual faculties? If it is the body's eye, then dreams are a species of hallucination; if it is the mind's eye, then dreams are a species of image.[1] These are very different theories, given the sharp distinction I have been insisting upon, and it is not obvious which of them is correct.

I shall be arguing that dreams are images, not percepts, but the matter is by no means straightforward.

It might be asked why I am assuming that images and percepts are the only potential candidates here. Couldn't there be a third type of experience that dreams are? Might not this category simply be—dreams? I have resisted assimilating images to percepts, insisting on an irreducible duality, so why can we not expand our taxonomy to take in a third major category? Perhaps dreams have their own distinctive characteristics, similar to images and percepts in some ways, but different in other ways. Indeed, at first sight they do seem like a kind of emergent hybrid of percept and image, neither fully one nor the other: they have all the force of perception, yet they are shot through with imaginative fantasy. Now, it is not that this theory can be ruled out dogmatically, but I think we do better to start with a more conservative approach and ask whether we *can* do justice to the phenomena without postulating a third *sui generis* experiential category. And I believe we will see that we can provide an illuminating and explanatory account of the constitution of dreams without tripling our experiential categories. Moreover, it would be odd if the faculties recruited in dreaming were not already exploited during waking life—as if the relevant faculties only spring into operation when the rest of the mind has shut down. Isn't it more natural to suppose that daydreaming and night-dreaming share their psychological architecture (or building blocks)? If you want to design a dreaming mind, it is certainly simpler to exploit faculties that already have a place in the mental economy (if that is not too clinical a term here). Finally, I am actually not convinced that there *could* be a third category—that images and percepts don't exhaust the possibilities. The distinctions I listed in Chapter 1 are dichotomous in nature, so it is hard to see how anything could fail to fall into one or the other basket. To be sure, we seem to be able to envisage the possibility of detaching some of the marks from others, so that we can contemplate the possibility of a type of experience that is (say) involuntary and yet attention-dependent, or both occlusive and non-observational.[2] But this is still not yet a case of an experience that is neither imagistic nor perceptual, since we may just be recombining contingent features of images and percepts. I have no proof that images and percepts, as characterized in Chapter 1, exhaust the possibilities, but I suspect they do, and anyway there are other reasons to restrict ourselves to the more conservative approach. The time to countenance a third experiential category would be if we failed to accommodate the data within the categories already on the table— and I don't think it will come to that.

I shall first set out some reasons for favoring the image theory over the percept theory; then I shall address some prima facie problems. I should note that these reasons are not of the apodictic variety, but together I think they constitute a good circumstantial case for the image theory.

1. The Observational Attitude

If dreams were hallucinatory percepts, they would generate, or be accompanied by, an observational attitude. While (unknowingly) hallucinating a conversation between two people, one will find oneself straining to hear better what is being said and orienting one's eyes so as to gain the best possible view. Widening the eyes and turning the head are likely concomitants. One opens one's senses to the progress of events, focusing one's attention accordingly. These are the behavioral and psychological marks of the acts of looking and listening, and percepts are tied in with these acts. But no such acts, outer or inner, accompany the dream: the eyes are shut, the head still; there is nothing in the nature of looking and listening going on. Nor is it that the sleeper is temporarily paralyzed. Rather, the experience is decoupled from these active systems; the observational stance is simply inappropriate. In fact, the dreamer is very like the daydreamer in her bodily attitude and indifference to her surroundings; she is preoccupied with what is transpiring within, not with what might be gleaned externally. The dream experience does not prompt any marks of interest in the dreamer's surroundings; hence there is no attempt to gain information about those surroundings. This suggests that the dreamer is hearing with the mind's ear when auditory experiences occur in the dream, not employing the body's ear in hallucinatory mode—for then she would be listening to what sounds might be picked up in the proximity of her ears. But she is no more using her ears in this way than I am when I voluntarily hear a tune in my head; indeed, I *stop* listening for what may come my way in such a case, so that I can concentrate better on my auditory imagery. And just as I close my eyes to enhance my visual imagery, so I keep them closed during the dream. I don't open them in an effort to get a better look, as I would if I were suffering from a daytime hallucination. So the image theory fits the data better in this respect.[3] Of course, it might be said that the dream percept is of a very special kind, in which these observational attitudes have been systematically removed; but this is ad hoc, and raises questions about the mechanisms and purpose of such removal—as well as dubiously denying the constitutive nature of the connections between percepts and looking and listening. The image theory is certainly simpler and less theoretically disruptive. So it has the advantage in accounting for the data.

2. Concurrent Imagery

Percepts and images do not compete with each other: you can have a visual image at the same time as having a visual percept (except in the case in which they have the very same content). Then, if dreams consisted of percepts, it ought to be possible to form images concurrently with undergoing the dream experience. If I am dreaming that I am surfing, having suitable visual experiences of the sea and the sky, then it ought to be possible to have an image of the Eiffel Tower at the same time—on the assumption that the surfing experiences are perceptual in nature. For, if I were wakefully hallucinating surfing, then there would be no more reason not to have such an image than if I really were surfing. If dreams were a series of hallucinatory percepts, then they could be accompanied by that other stream of imagery that accompanies waking percepts. The dream consciousness would admit of that two-dimensionality I mentioned earlier—percept accompanied by disparate image.[4] But there is no such double stream of visual experience during the dream: it is one-dimensional. There is just the dream experience itself, with no concurrent (and disparate) imagery.

We have to be careful about what this claim amounts to: it is not the claim that I cannot dream that I am having an image of the Eiffel Tower while surfing; it is the claim that I cannot have the experience of surfing in the dream and at the same time have in my consciousness an image of the Eiffel Tower.[5] We seem to be able in principle to dream absolutely anything—the *contents* of the dream can be anything. What I am saying is that *while having* the dream we cannot form an image of something else. But it is a familiar experience to imagine one thing while having a percept of another. If dreams were hallucinations, they could be accompanied by such simultaneous images, since the imaginative faculty would not be recruited by the dream—only the perceptual faculty would. But if dreams consist of images, then we would predict that no concurrent images could be formed, since the imaginative faculty is already being used. Just as images compete with one another in waking consciousness, so in dreams they compete—and the result is a single stream of experiential contents. There are no perceptual experiences during the dream, only imagistic ones, and so it is impossible to form a parallel series of images that cohabit with the dream images. Just as I can have only one daydream at a time, because of capacity limits on the imaginative faculty, so I can have only the dream experience—with no other contemporaneous exercises of imagination.

Granted that images are attention-dependent, we can explain some other features of dream consciousness. The mind can wander from its percepts into other mental domains—thoughts, images—since percepts are not attention-dependent. Percepts are sustained by something other than the attention. But the mind cannot wander from its images and expect the images to survive their fall from focal awareness. Now, in the case of dreams, I think it is obvious that mind wandering is not feasible: one does not find one's mind straying from what is currently being dreamed; the attention is rapt, captive. Of course, you can dream *that* you are looking at something while your mind is wandering; my point is that you cannot, within the dream consciousness, both have an experience as of such-and-such (say, surfing) and at the same time find your mind wandering to some other topic (say, what to do about that dent in your car). The reason for this is that the dream has already used up your attentive faculties, so there is no room left for other attentive acts—just as the image theory predicts. Just as your mind cannot wander from your daydreams and expect them to proceed by themselves, so it cannot wander from your dream images—and the reason in both cases is the attention-dependence of the imagination. This explains the *enthralling* character of dreams, the single-mindedness of the dream state. It is not that dreams are somehow intrinsically fascinating, so gripping that you cannot take your mind off them; on the contrary, they can be quite boring in the retelling. It is that they de facto have a monopoly on the attention. Since they are constituted by the attention, they are not the *kind* of thing from which the attention might wander. Their fascination for the dreaming consciousness is therefore an artifact of their constitutive nature, not a reflection of the narrative powers of their author. The reason why dreams don't bore the dreamer to the point that his mind goes off in search of more interesting material—as percepts may easily do—is simply that this would be tantamount to destroying the dream; the dream cannot therefore grind boringly on as the attention finds more fascinating subjects of contemplation.[6] It can never be hard to pay attention to one's dreams simply because they have no existence independently of the attention.

Their spellbindingness is a reflection of their very structure, not of the genius of their content; the dream author simply has a captive audience.

This is also why dreams strike us as "modally exhaustive"—I mean, why the dream world seems the only conceivable world during the course of the dream.[7] For, since the imagination is already fully occupied, we cannot use it to conjure up alternative imaginary worlds to that depicted in the dream. And perhaps this also accounts for their peculiar ability to *defeat* the dreamer's consciousness, to reduce him to despair—for no alternative to the presently experienced world can be envisaged. In waking consciousness I can be perceiving one thing and imagining something else: there is the perceived world and the imagined world. I "live" in both worlds, the actual and the possible, in that both are mentally represented by me. But in the dream there is only the dream world and no envisaged alternative to it; so I feel condemned to that world, since I can picture no other. I become modally blind, so to speak; the possible world I am conjuring in my dream is the only world that I can represent.[8] The sense of alternatives has disappeared from my consciousness. The thought "I might not have been having this experience" does not belong in the dream consciousness. This is predictable from the image theory and mysterious for the percept theory.

3. Wakefulness and Perception

When we go to sleep our senses switch off; we become "unconscious." We are no longer aware of what is going on around us. But according to the percept theory of dreams, our sensory apparatus becomes active again during dreams; we start to have experiences as of a surrounding world—except that these experiences are hallucinatory, non-veridical. But doesn't this sound wrong, taken literally? How can I start having the very same type of experiences, subjectively considered, during unconscious sleep that I have while awake and conscious? Wouldn't the onset of such experiences *wake me up*? Indeed, isn't the having of such experiences what being awake *consists in*? Obviously, waking hallucination does not confer unconsciousness on a person; you can be as awake while hallucinating as you are while veridically perceiving. So how can you have subjectively indistinguishable states and yet be asleep and unconscious? How can your consciousness have the same *structure* during dreaming sleep that it has when you are wide awake—with only the presence of an external stimulus as the difference?

When the perpetually hallucinating brain in a vat goes to sleep, there is a change in its state of consciousness; life is *not* one long dream to this subject of consciousness. The dreaming brain in a vat is in a different state of consciousness from the waking (but hallucinating) brain in a vat. But the percept theory has nothing to say about this difference: the dream is just more of the same—more hallucination. This seems wrong: the dreaming brain in a vat is in a qualitatively different state of mind from that which it is in when awake—or else it would be awake then too! Suppose I have taken a drug and am hallucinating liberally; I want to put an end to this state of mind, so I try to go to sleep. Don't I succeed if I do go to sleep? Doesn't sleep precisely put an end to sensory hallucination, as it does to ordinary veridical perception? It's not that I merely replace one type of hallucination with another. But the percept theory cannot accept this piece of common sense, since it takes sleep to be just the beginning of exactly the same type of state of consciousness. It says that dreaming sleep is simply waking percepts without actually being awake, as if wakefulness were something tacked extrinsically onto the percept.[9] But this idea sounds fishy: the perceptual consciousness seems precisely to *be* the waking consciousness.

Percepts necessarily incorporate a purported awareness of one's immediate surroundings; it strikes the perceiver that things are a certain way in his vicinity. During sleep we suppose that such a mode of consciousness has been terminated: it is not that the sleeper still has a purported awareness of his surrounding space—so that he is very wrong about the condition of his *bedroom*. That would be characteristic of a waking hallucination, which *points* (to speak) at the surrounding space. Rather, his consciousness no longer essays any such perceptual representation, since he is now unconscious; his mind is not *aiming* to get it right about his current environment. This is why it sounds so wrong to convict the dream of *malfunction*, as if it were in the business of telling the sleeper how things are around him, but dismally fails in this effort. Notice here how images cannot be so convicted either: they are not malfunctions of the sensory system but a different type of mental act altogether. The dream, like the image in general, represents *a* space, but it is not in the business of pointing to the neighboring space and telling us how it is there. But a hallucination is in precisely that business. And surely this is part of what it means to be awake.[10]

Is there any comparable tension between having images and being unconscious? I think not. Sleep shuts down the senses; correctly representing one's surroundings is no longer the concern of the sleeping mind. But there is no similar intuition that sleep shuts down the imagination. I close my eyes to imagine better, and I do the same in order to sleep. Forming images is not something that constitutively implies wakefulness, because it does not involve a purported awareness of one's surroundings; there is no *presence* built into it. So it is perfectly natural to suppose that images can occur during sleep. Thus images pass this test for being what dreams are made of.

4. Recognition

A striking fact about dreams is that we almost invariably know who and what we are dreaming about. And this knowledge does not arise through any procedure of inference from appearances to identities. It is not that someone in my dream presents the appearance of person A and so I infer that it is A I am dreaming about; I "just know" that it is A who is in my dream. This contrasts with identity knowledge derived from waking perception: here I do have to move from the appearance to the identity, via some sort of stored identity judgment. Hence there is fallibility built into the procedure, stemming from the fact that appearances can be deceiving. Now, if dreams were just hallucinatory percepts, our knowledge of the identity of our dream objects would take the same form: I judge that I am dreaming of A because someone with the appearance of A has cropped up in my dream. And this would seem to leave room for the possibility of mistake. By contrast, knowledge of the objects of imagining is not so based. It derives rather from stipulation, from the underlying intention. I imagine whom I *intend* to imagine. So this property of dreams—the non-recognitional character of the identity knowledge contained in them—fits nicely with the image theory. The reason we "just know" who we are dreaming about is that our knowledge comes from an underlying intention of some sort (of what sort I shall discuss later).

This account also accommodates something that the percept theory has great trouble explaining: how we can know the identity of our dream objects even when their appearance is grossly distorted. I may be dreaming about A, and know this in the dream, even though A looks totally different from the way she looks in real life (maybe she looks like B in the dream). So I cannot be inferring the identity from the appearance (or else I would judge that it is B I am dreaming about). But this is easily explained by the image theory, since there is nothing to stop me deciding to form an image of A that distorts her appearance in various ways. I can keep track of whom I am imagining because I know what my intention is: to form a distorted image of A.

In waking perceptual experience there is a constant stream of recognition judgments as percept meets memory: "Oh, old Smith is here again"; "There goes that guy I saw last week at the gym"; "She looks familiar." Recognition is one of the salient facts of ordinary conscious life (even if it is so automatic that we seldom pay attention to it). But I suggest that in dreams this kind of recognitional experience simply does not occur—any more than it does in daydreams. The identity of the objects is *given,* presupposed, implicit. We just take it for granted who we are dreaming about; there is no "shiver of recognition" when *she* strolls unannounced into your hitherto uneventful dream. That it is she is simply part of the fabric of the dream experience. Thus, "I had a dream about you last night" has an authority that "I saw you last night" does not have—and which "I formed an image of you last night" also has.[11]

5. *Narrative*

Dreams may often be chaotic, baffling, and pointless, but they do typically have a narrative structure, of varying degrees of coherence. They often have a beginning, a middle, and an end; they always seem to have some affective component. In my experience, they may have a denouement that must have been foreshadowed at the outset, since the whole point of the earlier sections often emerges only in the later sections (this is particularly true of anxiety dreams).[12] They are very often expressive of some concern that afflicts waking life. We need not follow the excesses of Freud and company in order to acknowledge that the dream is a medium of creativity, a meaningful sequence of related elements. The dream has *design.* But how can the percept theory account for this? The coherence of percepts is typically owed to the nature of the stimuli that elicit them—the actual course of external events. But in the dream all is said to be hallucination, so the coherence cannot come from outside. It must come from some sort of internal narrative source—the dream designer. But how can *percepts* be manipulated by such an internal agency? Aren't they the wrong kind of thing to be organized by an internal creative dream designer? I certainly cannot make my waking percepts susceptible to my creative whims; they refuse to be shaped by my plans for them (they are not subject to my will at all). So how can the narrative shaping that is characteristic of dreams be made to square with their alleged status as percepts?

MINDSIGHT

The image theory, by contrast, fits the bill perfectly: images can be shaped into narrative sequences, as they are in the case of daydreams. Images are subject to the will, and they are ideal items with which to patch together an inner story. Images, indeed, are a natural mental accompaniment to reading a story. Images and stories are made for each other. The dream designer merely needs to concatenate them together into a satisfying sequence. Percepts, by contrast, belong with the sober and factual. They purport to reflect what is actually happening out there in the mundane world.[13]

6. Saturation

Images can have blank portions, as I pointed out in Chapter 1; not everything is "filled in." I think the same is true of dream experiences: they can be more like sketches than fully realized representations. I once had a dream about a woman whose face was really only filled in around the mouth area (large red lips), the rest of the face being left pretty much blank (I knew quite well who she was); and this kind of sketchiness seems common in dreams. Both images and dreams can be "unsaturated" in the sense earlier explained. But the same is not true of percepts, even the hallucinatory kind: every point in the sensory field is filled in, occupied by some quality or other. So the percept theory does not fit the "incompleteness" of the dream experience, while the image theory fits it perfectly. Dreams vividly incorporate significant details, but they are lazy about insignificant ones—unlike percepts, and like daytime images. (This has a lot to do with the affective background of the image as opposed to the percept.)[14]

Let me here make an observation about the common statement that dreams can be only "black and white." I doubt that the people who say this mean it literally; what I think they mean is that dream images can be visual and yet colorless, or at any rate highly muted. This is not because they are determinately black and white through and through, but because the dream image has simply not been filled in with respect to color, or has been filled in only very minimally. The image can be highly selective in the features it builds in, and the color of an object may not be important to the image-making intentions of the imaginer—so the color might simply be left blank, a matter of indifference. I suspect that the loose talk of black and white dreams is (sometimes?) a reflection of this fact about images: sometimes the color of a dream object is not significant to the dreamer and is therefore left unspecified. The object is thus experienced as colorless, and then is loosely described as a case in which it is merely "black and white." (Of course, someone *might* really mean that a dream was purely black and white, and that these achromatic shades were strongly built into the dream image. Maybe so; but my conversations with sundry dreamers have tended to favor the idea of color neutrality instead.) It is a delicate question whether a visual image can be *totally* unspecific as to color—and I don't mean to take a firm stand on that question—but I think it is certainly true that the color of an imagined object can be, so to speak, unstressed or recessive, owing to its lack of relevance to the image maker's intentions and concerns ("I just want to form an image of a regular hexagon—I don't *care* what color it is!").

7. Imaginative Sensing

Although the senses are closed down during sleep, it may happen, especially during the transition to waking consciousness, that an outside stimulus is registered in some way—as when you hear your alarm clock as wedding bells in a dream you are having. The external stimulus gets incorporated into the dream by way of an interpretation of it that fits the content of the dream. I think this is a clear case of imaginative hearing: the imagination has imposed an "aspect" on the stimulus that is partly constrained by its acoustic character and partly pure fancy. If so, we have an exercise of imagination during the accompanying dream—a case of image and percept joining in an act of hearing-as. This favors the image theory of the dream. The only way to bend the data to the percept theory would be to maintain that in the alarm clock case the dreamer un-

MINDSIGHT

dergoes a perceptual *illusion*, comparable to the standard illusions of waking consciousness. Then, since such illusions are not exercises of imagination but distortions of the sensory systems, it could be said that there is nothing distinctively imaginative about the kind of case I have cited. But surely this is highly implausible: the interpretation placed on the stimulus is far too creative and idiosyncratic to be merely a standard visual illusion—such as the Muller-Lyer illusion. And there will be no explanation of it at the level of bottom-up sensory functioning; it is not an effect of the stimulus and some general property of the sensory system. Rather, it reflects the high-level top-down preoccupations of the dreamer's mind— for example, his anxiety about getting married (or his hopes in that regard). It is too "penetrable" by the dreamer's thoughts and emotions to be a mere sensory illusion.[15] So, again, the image theory accommodates the data better than the percept theory.

8. Pre-sleep Images

Part of the folk psychology of sleep is that repetitive conjuring of an image can induce the sleeping state: you form an image of a sheep jumping a fence, say, and keep repeating it. The assumption is often made that this is sleep-inducing because of the repetitive and monotonous nature of the mental act; you are boring yourself into unconsciousness. But it is not obvious that this is the right theory; after all, compulsively repeating the same *thought* is not conducive to sleep—indeed, it may be the cause of the insomnia. Let me then speculatively propose another hypothesis: filling your mind with images in this way *simulates* the dreaming state and so readies the mind for sleep. You put your mind into a state resembling its state during sleep, and so the transition is eased. And this works precisely because dreaming is itself a series of images.[16] If dreaming were a series of hallucinations, then there wouldn't be the resemblance I am invoking.

This "theory" is confirmed by the well-known phenomenon of hypnagogic imagery. People often experience abundant imagery just before sleep, and this imagery is a natural prelude to dreaming. Why? The answer is that hypnagogic imagery models the dreaming state, thus providing an intermediate state of consciousness between waking perception and sleeping dreaming. If the percept theory were true, by contrast, then the natural prelude to sleep would be waking hallucination; but that is clearly not what we observe. Pre-sleep imagery is the closest we get to dreaming while awake, so we can use it to help us fall asleep. This may not be serious laboratory science, but I venture to suggest that it does have some explanatory power. It is another tiny piece of circumstantial evidence for the image theory of dreams.

The foregoing are some pretty good reasons to suppose that dreams consist of images, not percepts. But there are some problems that need to be addressed. The first, and most obvious, is that dreams do not appear to be subject to the will: we do not decide what to dream, but instead occupy the role of passive recipient. Dreams often do not go the way we would want, but we are powerless to alter their course; in this respect they seem more like percepts. Now, this point does not automatically defeat the image theory, even if accepted at face value, since we could always declare subjection to the will not to be a necessary condition of image-hood. Maybe it holds for all waking images, but the images of sleep are different; they are simply a species of image that cannot be voluntarily controlled.[17] But I don't think we need to take this line, and there are positive reasons not to, apart from theoretical simplicity. Also, it starts to become unclear by what right we call something an image if it is declared not to satisfy the usual conditions that images satisfy; the issue begins to seem purely verbal. So I think it is better to see if we can retain the willed character of all images and explain the appearances away.

It would be wrong to suppose that the sleeper is entirely passive, a complete non-agent; sleeping and acting are not incompatible. Thus we have sleepwalking and sleep-talking, adjustments of posture to avoid discomfort, small movements seemingly correlated with the content of the dream. There is much evidence of creativity during sleep, which suggests mental action of some sort—as with the scientist who wakes up with the solution in hand. Dreams give evidence of plot intentions, as they coherently unfold to some sort of denouement, so it seems that a creative agency is behind them—an invisible narrator (as I will show). And there are also clear cases in which dreams can be subject to the will: we have all had the experience of intentionally terminating a nightmare when it becomes too emotionally intense, and the rarer phenomenon of "lucid dreams" allows for voluntary control over the full course of the dream. So it is not that dreams are totally immune from voluntary control, or that the sleeper is necessarily a merely passive lump. Agency has not been fully relinquished during sleep. Still, the dream seems very much *less* subject to the will than waking images are. So can dreams simply *be* the operation of the usual daytime imagination during the night hours? Can it be the *same faculty* that operates in the waking and sleeping states, obeying the same basic rules?

Here I think we need to make a more radical (though hardly unheard of) suggestion: we need to distinguish the *audience* of the dream from the *author* of the dream—the dream consumer from the dream producer. That is, we need to postulate a "psychic split" in the dreaming mind, a division of the self. Suppose we do that. What results? Well, we can then suppose that the dream author operates in a way that is sealed off from the knowledge and awareness of the dream audience, so the intentions and mental actions that generate the dream are not open to the consciousness of the dreamer *qua* consumer. The dream producer is unconscious relative to the dream consumer. This will generate the *illusion* of psychological passivity: the audience is passive, not intentionally generating the dream, so it will *seem* as if the entire process is passive; but behind the scenes the producer is busy actively generating the images that are being passively consumed by the audience. In other words, the apparent passivity of the image results from assuming the position of the dream audience—and this is the position that is given to our consciousness during the dream. But it does not at all follow from this that the dream process is really unwilled, since there may be an agency that is operating unconsciously. In short, dream images are the product of an *unconscious will*. If that is so, then dream images are not counterexamples to the necessary condition of subjection to the will. All images *are* subject to the will, after all, but this may not be apparent to the consciousness of their recipient.[18]

Is this a good view on independent grounds? Clearly, there has to be *some* unconscious generative process behind the causation of dreams: they don't come from nowhere. The question is how much this process resembles the kind of causation we find for daytime images—causation by intentions, and reflecting emotions and desires. How agent-like must the cause be? I think the evidence suggests that it must be *very* agent-like. For the dream gives every sign of *intelligent design:* it looks like something that was planned and executed with intelligence, foresight, even cunning.[19] Dreams often have plot-like structures, with surprises and revelations; they seem shaped to suit the emotions and concerns of the dreamer; they draw upon recent experiences, as well as old memories. They seem, in short, very like a fictional genre—a certain type of storytelling.[20] (The old idea that dreams are messages from God or prophetic communications is no doubt false, but perhaps it attests to the fact that the dream carries the imprint of agency upon it—as if someone were trying to tell you something. And someone is, but it is simply another part of you.) But only intelligent designers can tell stories, not brute non-intentional (in both senses) causes. To be sure, dreams can be chaotic and baffling, but they generally have some sort of temporal progression and sense of connectedness; they are not just a series of random images. And since we know that human brains house agent-like entities in the production of daytime images, there is no reason of principle not to suppose that the images of dreams have a similar type of causation. The difference is that in the dream the actions of the agent are hidden; but the production process is essentially the same. The dream is willed, but the willing occurs in the context of a psychic split.

Of course, Freud postulated an unconscious agency in the performing of what he called "the dream-work," and in this respect I agree with him. But this does not commit me to the full panoply of Freudian theory—particularly to the idea of repression as the source of the unconscious. There is, however, a question to which Freud has some sort of answer and which is left hanging by my account, namely, *why* is there such a psychic split? Freud's answer is that it is because the unconscious contains dark and dangerous desires that must be repressed for the stability of the entire psyche. But if this idea is abandoned, there is certainly a question as to why in the dream the agent-like causal process assumes an unconscious form: Why isn't it just like the daydream case, in which the willed character of the image is available to the mind? Why is there an illusion of passivity? Why does the audience of the dream adopt a passive role? Why can't the consumer and the producer be unified?[21]

I suspect the answer will take us to the topic of the next chapter: the phenomenon of dream belief. In dreams we appear to believe what we dream, and accordingly experience the appropriate emotions. But it is far from clear that this would be possible if the true cause of our dreams were given to our consciousness during the dream; for then we would be alert to their status as intentionally caused images—and hence suspend belief. We do not believe our daytime images because we know that we intentionally produce them; so to secure belief, the causation must be hidden from the believer. I conjecture, then, that the psychic split occurs in order to pave the way for dream belief and its associated emotions. For some reason, we have a *need to believe* during the dream, and this requires the illusion of passivity. Why *this* is so I am not sure, but it does seem to be the case; so there is some rationale for the descent into unconsciousness that characterizes the production of dream images. It is not that we are afraid of the unconscious, as Freud would have it; rather, we have an urge to believe what we merely fantasize. We sometimes want our beliefs to hook up with our images as well as with our percepts (this type of hookup will be the theme of the next chapter and beyond).[22]

But there is still some work left to do in this chapter. I have found a way to defend the agency of the dream image, but there is another feature of dreams that seems to make trouble for the image theory of dream experience: the appearance of a visual field. I said in Chapter 1 that images do not come with a visual field, but doesn't it seem that in dreaming you are really *seeing* things? Isn't it *as if* you are having percepts? And isn't this why you can be afraid of what you are dreaming about? Don't the dream objects seem as if they are *there?* These questions anticipate the question of dream belief, the topic of the next chapter, but I want to make some brief remarks now. What I want to say is that there is an *illusion* of a visual field in the dream—or, better, a *delusion*. The first point to note here is the attention-dependence of the dream experience: we do not have the phenomenon of unnoticed aspects of the dream, or a division between the center and the periphery of the alleged visual field. Everything visual about the dream is equally a focus of attention (and similarly for the other sense modalities). There is no more to the dream than what we put into it—what we sustain by means of attention. There is no such thing as seeing something "out of the corner of your eye" in a dream, with your attention switching to a hitherto neglected part of your visual field; the sensory content of the dream is attentively uniform, homogeneous. This is why the dream image can have gaps and be indeterminate; it contains only such detail as attention permits.

What about *presence*—the sense that the intentional object is right there? When I form a daytime image of a tiger it is "posited as absent," so that I feel no fear; but when I dream of a tiger isn't it "posited as present," so that fear occurs? Again, I think this is illusory (or delusory), and reflects merely the fact of dream belief, not a phenomenological datum: there is a sense in which I believe that a tiger is before me, but it is not that it really *looks* to me as if there is a tiger there; it is not with me exactly as it would be if I were *seeing* a tiger. No spatial relation between the object and my body is represented in the dream experience—that is, between the tiger and my prone frame. Of course, I can dream *that* I am facing a tiger: but this is not a relation between my body as it then is, lying asleep in bed, and the tiger; it is a relation between the tiger and my body as represented in the dream. As I noted earlier, it is not that dream experience points to my actual environment and makes an erroneous claim about what is there. In regular perception my body awareness interacts with my awareness of external objects to generate an impression of spatial relatedness, but in the dream the intentional objects are not brought into coordination with an awareness of my body as it then is—for I *have* no such awareness during the dream. And this I think is the key: since I have no (conscious) body awareness during the dream—no proprioceptive percept that enters the dream's content—there is nothing to bring together with the material of the dream to generate an impression of presence. The tiger cannot be presented as present *to me,* because I have no perception of me. Since there is no self-location, there is no location of objects *relative* to the self. So any impression of presence must be illusory.[23]

But why is there such an impression, however illusory? I think I have already said: if there is no perception of self to anchor the representation of presence, there is also no perception of self to give substance to the representation of *absence.* When I form a regular daytime image, I have a proprioceptive percept that stands at the opposite pole to the object I am imagining: that object is not *here,* where *I* am. So the sense of absence depends on the bodily presence of the self, as what the object is absent *from.* The body is present in virtue of the proprioceptive percept, and the imagined object is "posited" as absent from *it.* But in the case of the dream, *there is no such proprioceptive percept,* and hence no contrast point; thus the object cannot be "posited as absent." But this lack of awareness of absence should not be construed as a positive awareness of presence. The intentional structure of the dream does not incorporate a representation of absence, for the reason just stated; but it does not at all follow that it incorporates an assertion of presence. The illusion of presence results from the absence of a representation of absence, to put it paradoxically.

And isn't this what the experience of the dream suggests? I feel fear before my dreamt-of tiger (as opposed to dreaming *that* I feel fear—which is quite consistent with not really feeling it), but the fear is not quite the same as what I would feel if I were *really* seeing a tiger. It is not literally true that I, the dreamer, take the tiger to be right next to me; if I did I might leap from the bed and run for the door! It is perhaps *as if* I have the experience of seeing a tiger, but it doesn't follow that I really have such an experience. Hallucinating a tiger would produce the affective and motor reactions characteristic of veridically seeing a tiger, since genuine presence would be written into the experience; but dreaming of a tiger doesn't produce these reactions—so there is a difference between the two cases.[24]

The way is then clear to accepting that dreams consist of images: there are good reasons to say this, and no decisive objections against it. (Even if my readers did not need such an elaborate defense of this claim, taking it to be obvious to begin with, I think we have learned something by articulating the reasons that lie behind our natural acceptance of the claim.) But before we move on to the tricky problem of dream belief, I need to mention one further possibility, if only for completeness: the idea that dreams might consist of experiences of imaginative sensing. That is, dreams are made up of episodes of seeing-as (hearing-as, etc.)—combinations of percepts and images. On this view, there is an experiential core to the dream of genuine hallucination (the percept) overlaid with an exercise of imagination (the image). The sensory system yields up a non-veridical percept, and the imaginative faculty adds its input to the mix. Some dreams do indeed seem to work rather like this, as with the case of the alarm clock and the wedding bells: an external stimulus penetrates the sleeper's awareness and is then interpreted in the light of an ongoing dream; the resulting experience seems part percept and part image. The suggestion, then, is that it is always this way, except that the percept is endogenously produced and has no corresponding external stimulus (it's a pure hallucination).[25]

Now, this view is certainly contrived and complicated, but it is not intrinsically absurd. It accommodates the reasons I cited for favoring the image theory, since it proposes an image component to every dream experience, and it might claim to supply a dose of phenomenal substance to the pure image theory—injecting some strength and vividness into the somewhat pallid pure image.[26] But I think there is no good reason to accept the imaginative sensing theory of the dream, as opposed to the simple image theory, and some considerations against it. We can account for all the data within the terms of the pure image theory, so there is no need to complicate the story. Nor does there appear to be the kind of duality in the dream experience that the imaginative sensing theory implies: the experience doesn't bifurcate into a perceptual core and an imaginative overlay. Furthermore, it is hard to see how to construct a narrative from core percepts as the raw materials, since they are not capable of manipulation in the ways simple images are; percepts would tie the dream-work down. And if dreams were percept/image hybrids, they would carry some of the marks of the percept— such as engaging the observational attitude and implying wakefulness. But, as we saw, these are not acceptable consequences. In the light of these points, then, the pure image theory is to be preferred. The imaginative sensing theory of the dream deserves to be added to the list of possibilities—it exists in logical space—but it doesn't look like a very attractive way to account for the data. The next and pressing question is whether the image theory can account for the phenomenon of dream belief.

Dream Belief

Mental images do not, in general, invite belief. If, in the course of a daytime reverie, I form an image of myself in Paris, I have no tendency to believe that I am in Paris. I am well aware that I am entertaining a mere image. The image system and the belief system are insulated from each other. In this respect images differ markedly from percepts, which do invite belief: except in special circumstances, I will believe that I am in Paris if I have perceptions to that effect.[1] Percepts afford reasons for belief, but images do not; there is an evidential relation in the one case but not in the other. This seems perfectly clear, and perfectly intelligible. But in the case of dreams this simple picture seems radically subverted: for in dreaming we do on the face of it believe what we dream, and dreams (as we have seen) consist of images. How can this be? How is dream belief *possible?* Sartre, who also holds that dreams are images, is acutely aware of this problem, writing: "We will certainly be asked: how does it happen that you can believe in the reality of dream images since it is you yourself who construct the dream as images. Their intentional nature as images should exclude every possibility to believe them to be realities."[2] The problem may be put this way: The nature of the image is such that it is evident to the imaginer that she is having an image (not a percept), because there are a number of marks that distinguish the image and are accessible to the imaginer—those I have listed earlier. Thus you cannot *fail* to tell the image from its distant relative, the percept; and if so, you will not be inclined to believe what you merely imagine. Yet in the dream we seem more than ready to let our beliefs be shaped by our dreams. So how can dreams be made up of images? How can we be so blind to, or dismissive of, their status as mere images—those harbingers of nothing actual?

It would be a mistake to suppose that we have already resolved this problem in the previous chapter by assigning the agency behind the dream to the unconscious. This does indeed allow us to understand how the willed character of the dream might be concealed from the audience of the dream—since it is unconscious—and hence how this cue to the nature of the dream as image might be inaccessible. But there are many other distinguishing marks that are not hidden in this way, so the question must still arise as to how we manage to make the kind of mistake we appear to be making—namely, confusing images with percepts. The lack of a visual field by itself ought to be a sufficient cue that we are confronted by images, not percepts. And the fantastic quality of so many dreams ought to alert us to the fact that they cannot be trusted: the world of the dream simply does not comport with what we independently know to be true.[3] So again, how are we capable of making such a gross error? It is like confusing pains with tickles or visual percepts with auditory ones. A clear phenomenal difference appears unaccountably neglected. This is the problem of dream belief.

Let me mention some easy ways out that don't really cut the mustard. The simplest response is to deny that there is any phenomenon to be explained: we don't form anything like beliefs in our dreams. There is nothing in the nature of assent or acceptance; we are "doxastically neutral" with respect to the content of our dreams. Maybe we are even incredulous: we positively disbelieve what our dreams contain. We no more believe our dreams than we believe our daytime reveries; our doxastic state is the same in the two cases. This response is surely much too simple. One obvious way in which dreams differ from mere reveries is the connection to emotion: we can be afraid in a dream in a way we never are when merely daydreaming. We are simply not *detached* from the dream in the way this response suggests. We simply do give our assent to what we dream.[4]

More plausibly, it might be said that our dream beliefs come in a relativized form: what I believe is that *in the dream world* I am about to be attacked by a tiger; I don't believe that in the *real* world this is my condition. (This would be like believing that in possible world *w* I can fly but not in the actual world.) On this view, I do not make the mistake of confusing my dream images with percepts, because percepts are what warrant beliefs about the *real* world, and my beliefs concern only the world of the dream. Now, aside from the obscurity of this notion of "belief with respect to the dream world," and the residual question of how mere images could warrant even that type of belief, there is an obvious problem here: dream beliefs can conflict with ordinary beliefs, but these relativized beliefs don't conflict (that is the whole idea). I may dream that I am about to be attacked by a tiger, forming the corresponding belief; when I wake up I experience relief that this is not so. But that would not be possible if the beliefs did not conflict. So dream beliefs must be the usual type of unrelativized belief: I simply believe in the dream that I am about to be attacked by a tiger. This is why my emotions are as they are during the dream.[5]

Next, someone might invoke the notion of "make-believe" or "pretend belief."[6] I don't really *believe* anything in my dreams; rather, I *make* believe that things are thus and so—as a child may make believe that he is playing with a gun. The trouble with this theory, as stated so far, is that it is too weak: you don't wake up in a cold sweat if you are merely *pretending* you are about to be attacked by a tiger. There has to be more to it than that (in fact, I think this view is on the right track, but it needs development and supplementation). The *seriousness* of dream belief must be captured, and the idea of make-believe cannot, as it stands, do that; the dreamer is not merely *playing* at belief.

In reply to this, it might be said that the condition of the dreamer is one of extreme *credulity:* he is like someone who takes superstitions seriously, who is evidentially irresponsible. Images provide no good evidence for the corresponding belief, but the dreamer has become extremely gullible, a doxastic patsy—he will believe anything. The trouble with this is that even the most gullible believer will draw the line at believing his images. Where is the uncritical *naif* who believes what he sets himself to imagine? What kind of credulity could lead a person to believe that he is in Paris simply because he has imagined it? That is more like insanity than credulity (as I will show). We need some other account of the dreamer's state of mind.[7]

At this point the reader may feel that it is time to give the percept theory another chance, and indeed I think that the problem of dream belief is the best reason there is for looking with favor on that theory. For that theory seemingly provides a straightforward explanation for dream belief: we believe our dreams because our dreams consist of percepts, and percepts are the kind of thing that really warrants belief. The dreamer is therefore not confused or irrational; he believes what he does on good evidence—it is just that all his percepts are hallucinatory. The dreamer has robust belief states for the simple reason that he bases them on percepts (albeit hallucinatory ones), just as he does in waking life. This sounds attractively simple, but there are two big problems. First, the percept theory is false, as we have seen. Second, on closer examination we can see that it doesn't remove the underlying puzzle, because the beliefs formed during dreams conflict with *other* beliefs we have— and yet this doesn't inhibit their formation. I have a whole set of beliefs about my position in the world, and these will contradict what a given dream leads me to believe—but I believe the dream nonetheless. Suppose my dream experiences give me evidence for the belief that p, yet all the rest of my experience, gathered during waking hours, strongly supports the belief that not-p. The belief that not-p is extremely well confirmed and a part of my system of belief that I am rightly very reluctant to give up; and yet my dream tells me that p. What am I to believe? Since the dream is relatively isolated, and hence only weakly supports the belief that p, I should persist in my well-confirmed belief that not-p. But I don't; I instantly and without any hesitation believe that p. I don't even worry about its inconsistency with the rest of my experiences and beliefs. But this can't be right: if I am simply forming beliefs on the basis of evidence, I ought not to rush to belief in this way. The problem is how my dream beliefs can *coexist* with my regular beliefs; and the percept theory doesn't solve this problem, it exacerbates it. We still don't know how dream belief is possible. True, the beliefs come out rational relative to their basis in the dream experience, but they come out irrational relative to other beliefs. The lump has reemerged at another point under the carpet. What we need is a theory that explains how dream beliefs can coexist with images *and* with other conflicting beliefs.

The best way forward now is to make a list of all the belief phenomena that occur in dreams, so that we know what we have to accommodate; once we have assembled the data, we can ask what theory best explains them.

1. Tolerance of Inconsistency

I believe that I live in America, and this belief persists overnight. Suppose I dream that I live in England, and that I form the corresponding belief. Do I revise my earlier belief in the light of my new belief? Do I stop believing that I live in America? I think this is implausible. I certainly have no *experience* of such belief revision; I don't say to myself, "I could have sworn I live in America, but now

I'm persuaded that I live in England." I form the new belief without even considering the old one. It is as if I am indifferent to it. This suggests that I keep the old belief and simply add the new one, despite their inconsistency. The two beliefs are somehow insulated, and the inconsistency tolerated. And notice how very inconsistent they are: the very same proposition, identically represented, is believed and disbelieved—identical reference, identical sense, identical language even. The case is even more extreme than in Saul Kripke's puzzle about belief, since in that case London is experienced differently in the circumstances of belief formation, and the languages are different.[8] In the dream case it is really as if I have two different believers inside my head. How is this possible? How can such contradictory beliefs coexist in the dreamer's mind? And notice that, upon waking, I will bring my old belief back to mind and revise my dream belief—and I do have an experience of *this,* since I may feel great relief that what I believed in my dream is not actually true. At this point the inconsistency becomes manifest to me, while before I seemed not to be perturbed by it.[9] Am I just fantastically irrational during sleep? Does the simplest logic escape me? Do I suffer from amnesia during the period of the dream?

2. Selective Quasi-amnesia

I clearly "forget" many things in the course of a dream; they are put aside and ignored. It is not that I suffer from actual amnesia during the dream, but the dream is selective as to which of my memories it chooses to incorporate. There are things I know quite well that do not come into the dream—as when I dream that I can fly. But I don't forget everything, of course; all sorts of information that I possess enter into the construction of the dream. I dream of flying over England and remember where London is located and that it is the capital. So my "amnesia" is selective: some of the content of the dream is invented (in violation of the known facts) and some is based on reality. Some of my memory beliefs are active in the dream, and some are bracketed. This bracketing of belief needs to be explained.

3. Coherence

Although dreams can be fragmented and confusing, there is typically an internal coherence in the story they tell; so the beliefs I form within the dream tend to be themselves coherent. I don't find myself holding contradictory beliefs *within* the dream. Instead, the dream experiences give expression to a world that follows some sort of regularity, however different it may be from the real world. This is part of the narrative structure of the dream.

4. Action and Emotion

The beliefs I form during the dream are disconnected from action and linked to emotion. I dream I am about to be attacked by a tiger: I feel the emotion of fear, but I don't make a move—I just lie there. The belief has triggered my affective system, but it has left my motor system in a state of passivity. Waking belief is connected to both in the obvious way—the fear gives rise to the action—but the dream belief produces emotion without action. Why don't my emotions correlate with the expected actions? And in those cases in which we find a kind of incipient and truncated action—a twitching of the leg muscles while dreaming of running for your life— why is it that we don't get the full motor response?[10] This too needs to be explained.

5. Quasi-emotion

Although we obviously do feel emotions during dreams, and on occasion for some time after waking up, there seems to be a qualitative difference between these emotions and their waking counterparts. True, I am terrified of that advancing tiger in my dream, but am I *as* afraid of it as I would be in real life? Am I afraid in exactly the same *way*? Correspondingly, do I believe in the tiger in exactly the same way in the dream as I would in real life? There is a *kind* of assent, as my emotions attest, but is it no different from regular assent? Intuitively, one wants to append a "quasi" to these psychological descriptions: I have *quasi*-fear, *quasi*-belief, et cetera. They are not quite the genuine article, though they approximate very closely. What is going on here? What is this mitigation of affect and assent?

6. Dream Ascent

It sometimes happens during dreams that one is struck with the recognition that one is only dreaming. The dream may be either very good or very bad, and a little voice inside whispers, "It's only a dream"; thereupon one wakes up. Normally, of course, one is absorbed in the dream and does not entertain the possibility that it is just a dream; but there are occasions on which the status of the dream is revealed during its course. Once this condition of "dream ascent" is reached, the dream beliefs lose their hold—they are abandoned. The dream is deemed unworthy of assent, despite its power to instill belief earlier. When the judgment that it is only a dream is made, the dream beliefs melt away. Again, we need some account of this phenomenon.

Perhaps the theory I am about to suggest has already dawned on the reader; I certainly formulated the foregoing points with that theory in mind. It is essentially the theory proposed by Sartre, though with some additions and refinements (and clarity, I hope).[11] I call it the *fictional immersion* theory. The basic idea is that the dream is a story—a piece of fiction—told in sensory terms (images), in which the dreamer becomes unusually deeply immersed. It is this notion of immersion that does the work. The dreamer becomes so absorbed in the dream story that his responses mimic what he would think and feel if really witnessing the events in question. This notion of absorption or immersion is familiar to us in more diluted forms, as in our response to fictional works of different types—theatrical productions, films, novels, and so on.[12]

The idea, simply put, is that the attitudes we have in dreaming are just an extreme case of this. My aim in making this suggestion is not to produce a good theory of this type of immersion; it is to suggest that the state of dream belief is a special case of it, with some distinguishing marks. So I am going to assume that we have a good enough idea of the state of mind in question: it is simply that psychological state that overtakes us when we are thoroughly entranced by a story, in its grip. And my claim is that the dreamer is in this type of state with respect to the dream story generated from within him.

The attraction of this theory is obvious: it reconciles the image theory of dreams with the phenomenon of dream belief. While I am immersed in a novel, I am not under the strange delusion that the marks on paper are real events that I am observing; I know that I am only reading a book, not witnessing the events described in it. Nor do I mistake the images that form in my mind for belief-inviting percepts. Yet I am able to enter into the story to such a degree that my emotions may be stirred, rather *as if* I were witnessing these events. Perhaps even closer to the dream, when am I watching a film I do not confuse the images on the screen with real events; nor do I mistake my prompted imaginings for reality.[13] Yet I may find myself so absorbed that my state of mind mimics real belief and feeling; I "enter into" the story. Similarly, in a dream I am not under the illusion that the images are percepts—I am implicitly aware (in some sense) that they are not—yet I am able to enter into the dream fiction in such a way as to become emotionally affected. I am not confused about the status of dream experiences; it is just that the dream images can draw me into a fictional world in such a way as to engage my cognitive and affective faculties. So engrossed am I by the dream story that I give my assent to it—or go into a state that is very similar to ordinary assent. Fictional immersion simulates belief.[14]

But is this kind of immersion enough? Don't I believe my dreams more strongly, more stubbornly, than I "believe" what I read when absorbed in a novel or see when carried away by a film? Aren't my emotions more like the real thing? I "believe" that the actor on the stage is about to stab the other actor, but do I *believe* it? I think this is a very reasonable question, and I propose to answer it with two points, the second a good deal more speculative than the first. The first is that there is an important difference between the ordinary case of fictional immersion and the dream case, namely that the intentional objects of the dreaming consciousness are the *only* intentional objects of the mind at that time. Consider reading a novel: you are perceptually aware of the words on the page, as well as of your bodily posture, and anything else that may fall within your sensory fields; and you are also aware, though not perceptually, of the people and places that the novel describes (for this you have to use your imagination). So there is the real world of perceived objects and the fictional world of imagined objects, and these run concurrently in your consciousness. There are two levels of intentionality, both of which are part of your total state of awareness. And the immersion you experience in one of these—the fictional world—is conditioned by your perception of the other— the artistic artifact. The perceived objects are always there to remind you that the fictional world is not the real world; they constitute a kind of limit on how immersed you can become. To get as immersed as possible, you try to shut down the sensory stimulation around you, but of course you can't stop seeing the letters on the page or the images on the screen—and these always function to keep you anchored in the real world. And the same is true of all fictional forms: the realm of fictional intentionality is mediated by the real world of perceptual intentionality, so that the immersion can never be complete; the fictional world can never be the *sole* field of intentionality for you. To become immersed in it you must always keep a grip on the perceptual world, but this very fact is what prevents full immersion.[15]

But in the case of dreams, the perceptual faculties are shut down; there is no field of perceptual intentionality to distract from the intentionality proper to the dream. The sole intentional objects are the objects dreamed about; your mind is wholly occupied in representing those objects. There is no reminder of the real world, contrasting with the world imagined. Hence the immersion can proceed unimpeded: your consciousness can be fully taken up with the world of the dream, with no perceptual world clamoring for the title of reality. The concept of reality drops out of the picture; there is no contrast between what is dreamed and what is perceived, because nothing is perceived. The prime obstacle to full fictional immersion in the waking state is therefore absent. It is as if you could read a novel without having to look at marks on a page, or experience a movie without having to gaze at a screen. In such a condition your mind would make direct unmediated contact with the events and objects of the story. Wouldn't this facilitate immersion enormously? In the dream, likewise, your mind is directed solely and immediately to the objects and events of the dream—so you can't help getting fully immersed. You sink into the dream, let it flow over you, with nothing to distance you from the events represented. This feature of the dream marks an important distinction between dream immersion and the ordinary waking kind of fictional immersion, and enables us to see how much deeper the immersion might go in the dream case.

The second, more speculative point concerns hypnosis. This may seem a strange subject to bring into the discussion, but, reader, bear with me—you never know what might emerge. The hypnotic state is essentially one of extreme *suggestibility:* the subject is exceptionally prone, sometimes laughably so, to believe and feel what the hypnotist suggests. The hypnotist exploits the subject's standing suggestibility to induce a state of heightened suggestibility; thus a transition is made to a state of mind in which beliefs are formed at the simple say-so of the hypnotist. My suggestion, then, is that the dreaming state is analogous to the hypnotic state: both are states of heightened suggestibility in which the usual guardedness in belief formation is suspended. We sometimes speak metaphorically of being "mesmerized" by a fictional production, meaning that it overtakes our entire consciousness, drawing us inexorably into the story; my suggestion is that we are mesmerized by our dreams—literally. The author of the dream acts upon us like a hypnotist: it is as if we had a hypnotist in our head, playing on our suggestibility, setting up all kinds of odd beliefs and emotions in us. Part of our mind puts the other part into a hypnotic trance.[16]

This sounds, I know, like a far-fetched idea, but let us try to consider it on its merits. First, the theory does have some explanatory power: it explains how dream belief can be as strong as it apparently is. Compare someone who is dreaming that his pants are on fire with someone who is convinced by the hypnotist that this is the case. There is an undeniable similarity here; and like effects tend to have like causes. Second, we can see from hypnosis how there are states of mind in which beliefs can be formed for palpably insufficient reasons, as a result of internal suggestibility rather than the weight of external evidence. Third, it would be odd if the hypnotic state were confined only to the influence of hypnotists; it is far more likely that they are tapping into a mental tendency that is there already. The phenomenon of suggestibility, more or less extreme, is certainly widespread, and has many manifestations apart from hypnotic trance. Why could it not also have a place in the sphere of dreams? Perhaps, indeed, it owes its *origin* to the dreaming mind—so that dreams are the primary site of suggestibility. Then it would be more correct to say that hypnosis resembles dreaming than vice versa.[17] And fourth, the hypnotist characteristically proceeds by simulating the state of sleep in the subject. He begins by focusing the subject's attention on his voice, thus shutting out other perceptual input. He tells the subject that she is "feeling sleepy" and that her eyes are closing. The subject appears to fall into a slumber. Then she is told to wake up and obey the hypnotist's commands. There is a glassy look in the subject's eye as she is induced to believe and feel a whole range of things without any basis in reality. And when the subject is finally told to snap out of it, she looks like someone awaking from a dream—bemused, relieved, not quite there yet. The process certainly resembles going into dreaming sleep, only the "dream" is in the hands of the hypnotist. Could it then be that the hypnotist is occupying the role usually occupied by the hidden dream-maker? He has tapped into the subject's dream mechanisms and hijacked them for his own ends.[18] Hypnotic suggestibility is dream suggestibility in the harsh light of day. Doesn't this hypothesis explain a lot?

The hypothesis has empirical consequences that might be checked. We could ascertain by brain scan whether the brain activity of the dreamer resembles that of the hypnotized subject: electroencephalograms, MRI, and so on. Perhaps there is a cerebral signature for increased suggestibility. We could also investigate whether mental imagery is increased during hypnosis, thus resembling the state of mind of the dreamer. Do the hypnotist's instructions elicit plentiful and potent imagery in the subject? If so, dream belief and hypnotic belief share a foundation in enhanced imagery. We certainly say of the haplessly hypnotized subject that he is "imagining things"—that his imagination has got the better of him. So the theory is not just a philosopher's speculation with no empirical content.

The point of this suggestion was to explain how it is that fictional immersion in the case of dreams could take such a powerful hold on the dreamer's psyche: it is because the immersion is accompanied by something akin to hypnotic trance (or better, the hypnotic trance is akin to the dreaming state—an odd by-product or outgrowth of our natural propensity to be seized by our dreams). If the suggestion is correct, then it is clear that the problem of dream belief can be resolved, since hypnotically induced belief seems to have all the power one could possibly want. Dream belief stems from fictional immersion *plus* extreme suggestibility. What we must do now is examine this theory in the light of the data I have itemized: is it consistent with the agreed data of dream belief?

I think it is easily seen that it is. Tolerance of inconsistency is essentially the same phenomenon that we find in ordinary cases of fictional immersion: I know very well that the actor on the stage is not about to stab the other actor, but I "believe" that he is. I become absorbed in a novel in which a certain world leader has been assassinated, but I know very well that he has not. I am hypnotized into believing that I am a barking dog, but part of me knows that this is rubbish. The dreamer's tolerance of inconsistency is therefore not some kind of preternatural irrationality or disregard for logic; it is simply the correlative of fictional immersion. Without fictional immersion the contradictions would be intolerable, but with it we get belief insulation. The correlative attitudes—of ordinary belief and the belief of fictional immersion—are not the *same* attitude, so they can be taken toward contradictory propositions. But they are close enough to generate many of the same affective and behavioral phenomena. Of course, this is not to give a *theory* of fictional immersion, and hence not a theory of this kind of belief inconsistency; it is merely to point out that we have other instances of such tolerance and that dream belief is a special case of it. In fact, I think it is very hard to provide a good theory of fictional immersion;[19] but I know that it exists, and I am trying to put it to work.

Selective quasi-amnesia is also exemplified in fiction: the author will include some known facts in his work but also alter others. When you read the story, you bring to bear your background knowledge, but you also delete such parts of it as do not fit the fiction—just as in the dream some knowledge is carried over and some is suspended or contradicted. Memory is selectively exploited in the fictional work, and in immersion in it. The dream is a story that preserves some truths but jettisons others, and is understood accordingly.

Stories typically possess internal coherence—the semblance of a plot, character constancy, elementary cause and effect. Maybe dreams are a more "experimental" form of fiction, with greater tolerance for jumble and the leap of faith, but they also have this kind of fictional coherence. The novel need not cohere with the real world, with actual history, but it does require some inner coherence of its own in order to engage with the reader's understanding; and the same is true of the dream: pure jumble is not what dreams are made of. Dreams have theme, narrative structure, emotional resonance—and hence invite fictional immersion. There is an *art* to the dream.[20]

Immersion in a work of fiction involves emotional responsiveness and motor disconnection. While you are reading a book or watching a film, your emotions may be running high—tears streaming down your face, heart racing, face flushed with joy—but you don't move much. It is as if your body knows it's just a story but your mind doesn't; your mind reacts as if the fiction is real, but your body is more skeptical. This is particularly true for the emotion of fear: that emotion may be rampant in you as you read or watch, but you don't head for the door. Emotion becomes detached from action. But isn't this what we find in the dream also? There you lie, immobile in your bed, not moving a muscle, and fear is coursing through you: the emotion is there all right, but it is cut off from its customary expression. Sometimes the audience of a fiction will evince a hint of the customary behavior—jumping when a sudden shock is administered, for example—and equally the dreamer may let slip such etiolated responses. But generally both states of consciousness involve a shutdown of the motor system, accompanied by affective activity.[21]

I noted earlier that dream fear is not *quite* the same as real fear; it doesn't have quite the *clout* of real fear. And dream belief is not quite as committed as ordinary belief; there is some kind of holding back or reservation about it. It is very hard to characterize exactly what this involves, but the point I want to make now is that the same kind of holding back applies to the emotions felt in ordinary fictional immersion. The belief and emotion of fictional immersion are *quasi*-belief and *quasi*-emotion (whatever this may ultimately come to). So there is a parallel here between the two cases: the "fictional stance" always introduces a modification into the psychological states at play, a kind of diminution or transformation. They are still recognizable as the usual emotions, but they appear in another guise—muted versions of themselves. The sadness of dreams is like the sadness we feel about fictional events: real enough, but not with quite the sting of real sadness.[22]

Dream ascent has its counterpart in the abrupt recognition that one is only witnessing a fictional work. The mother says to the petrified child, "It's only a movie," thereby jolting the child from a state of fictional immersion into a state of fictional ascent. The immersion may persist, but the ascent lessens its power to dominate the psyche. For the adult, raising the lights in the theater may induce a stepping back from the world of the fiction, inviting a judgment of fictional ascent—whereupon the emotions lately felt wane rapidly or instantly evaporate. For you cannot be both immersed in a fiction and consciously thinking "this is only fiction." Your attention cannot be both on the fictional work *qua* fictional artifact *and* on the fictional world depicted. In dream ascent you also step out of the dream fiction, thereby loosening its grip; the result is typically that you wake up, exiting the dream world entirely. The shedding of belief that this entails mirrors the psychological *volte-face* involved in explicitly recognizing a fictional work for what it is. In dreams, you cannot apply the concept of the dream if you wish to stay immersed; in "living" a work of fiction, you must not let your thoughts employ the concept of fiction.[23] That would take you outside what you need to stay within.

Perhaps it will be said that in exploiting these parallels between dreams and fictional works I am "explaining the obscure by the more obscure." The parallels are there, it will be admitted, and the dreaming state is genuinely analogous to the state of fictional immersion—but we understand so little about the latter state that no advance has been made. My reply to this should be obvious: I have been trying to show how dream belief is possible, and my strategy has been to identify other cases that display the structure implicit in dream belief. So the mere fact that dreams comprise images cannot be itself a reason to declare the problem of dream belief insoluble, since we have analogous situations elsewhere. Besides, that old maxim has little to be said for it: what we want is a *true* explanation with some explanatory power; that the *explanans* itself raises questions is not a reason to deny it legitimacy. I am making a kind of map of the imaginative mind, linking one place to another; I am not suggesting that every location is an oasis of clarity and theoretical order. My point here has been that the various phenomena of dream belief can be illuminatingly captured in terms of the fictional immersion paradigm. And when they are, the image theory of dreams can be reconciled with the fact that we believe what we dream.

Let me end this chapter with a more general point about belief and other psychological notions. We should not make the mistake of supposing that everything we call "belief" fits some chosen paradigm of belief—say, assenting to a sentence when confronted by a sensory stimulus. Beliefs come in a great many forms: everything from beliefs about perceived matters, to ethical beliefs, to theoretical beliefs, to religious beliefs ("faith"), to dream beliefs. Similarly, the umbrella concept of *desire* should not obscure the vastly many things that can be called by that name—everything from pangs of hunger to ethical motives. If we become fixated on one kind of case, we shall find ourselves withholding the name from other kinds of case—engaging in a kind of strict verbal policing (an occupational hazard of philosophers of a certain stripe). In this frame of mind, we might find ourselves doubting the idea of dream *belief*—as we compare it with some other instance of the concept. Thus if we focus on percept-driven beliefs, we may find ourselves skeptical of the notion of image-driven beliefs (and similarly for emotions, etc.). But we should resist this tendency and take the world as we find it. The case of dream belief simply shows us how broad and polymorphous the concept of belief is. The sure test that dreams are suffused with belief is their ability to generate emotions that are conditional on belief, such as fear and elation—with which dreams are full.

Delusion

8

I have distinguished two ways in which beliefs may be formed: as a result of perception in waking life, and in concert with imagery during dreams. In the case of perception the belief is caused by, and based on, the percepts that result from the operations of the senses. In the case of dreams, the belief is prompted by the images that result from the operations of the unconscious dream agent, through the mechanism of fictional immersion. Percepts control belief, but so in certain circumstances do images. In both cases the process may result in false belief—typically in the case of dreams, atypically in the case of perception (through illusion and hallucination). In this chapter I am concerned again with imagination-driven belief, and my thesis is that so-called delusion is a special case of it. That is, the psychic structure of daytime delusion resembles that of the dream. Madness is thus akin to the dream state. Dreaming is sleeping insanity; insanity is a waking dream—roughly speaking.

Consider delusions of persecution and of grandeur: how do they arise? Here is my proposed model of their etiology: The subject suffers from an emotional disturbance centering on anxiety or thwarted desires. This emotion stimulates the imagination, producing images of persecution or wish fulfillment. These images feed back to the emotions and inflame them further. A feedback effect ensues. The images come to be *believed* by the subject; hence the conviction of persecution or of grandeur. The essence of this simple model is that the delusional beliefs are generated by the imagination system, driven by the affective system, with all the distinctive characteristics we have observed. They are *not* generated by a malfunctioning perceptual system (i.e., by hallucinations and illusions). It is not that the senses are functioning abnormally and inviting belief in their erroneous deliverances; they may in fact be perfectly normal. The problem lies in an abnormality of the imagination as it links to belief. The pathology afflicts the imagination system, not the perceptual system. This distinction of psychological mechanisms follows directly from everything I have said so far, because I have sharply distinguished imagination from perception. To be misled by one's imagination is a very different matter from being misled by one's senses (as we saw in the case of dreams).

The idea that delusion is the product of a deranged imagination is by no means new. Hume writes:

> Nor will it be amiss to remark, that as a lively imagination very often degenerates into madness or folly, and bears it a great resemblance in its operations; so they influence the judgment after the same manner, and produce belief from the very same principles. When the imagination, from any extraordinary ferment of the blood and spirits, acquires such a vivacity as disorders all its powers and faculties, there is no means of distinguishing betwixt truth and falsehood; but every loose fiction or idea, having the same influence as the impressions of the memory, or the conclusions of the judgment, is received on the same footing, and operates with equal force on the passions.[1]

The delusions of madness, then, are traceable to a disturbance of the imagination: hence we speak of having an "overactive imagination" and of being "deceived by the imagination." Normally, our beliefs are detached from the imagination, and linked to perception; in madness our beliefs become shaped by the imagination, and perception loses its hold on them.[2] The point I want to insist on is that this is a very different theory from the idea that such delusions result from perceptual *hallucination*—since images and percepts are radically different types of mental state. It is not that in delusion beliefs stay connected to perception, which turns out to be hallucinatory. Rather, beliefs become decoupled from perception and attached instead to imagination—much as they do in dreams.

These exercises of imagination may consist of pure images or of episodes of imaginative sensing. Thus, in the latter type of case, the delusional paranoid may overhear an innocent conversation and imaginatively project on it a persecutory intent; she hears it *as* a conspiracy to harm her. She may also, of course, simply be visited by auditory images that have a persecutory content: she hears voices "in her head." In both cases the origin of the paranoid belief is the imagination, operating alone or in conjunction with the senses. Just as depression is a disorder of the affective system and amnesia is a disorder of the memory system, so delusion is a disorder of the imagination system—but *not*, according to my thesis, a disorder of the perceptual system. Of course, vagueness about the distinction between percepts and images will cause one to overlook the theoretical difference I am insisting on here, but my whole point so far has been to stress this distinction; I am now bringing the distinction to bear on the characterization of the delusions of madness.[3]

I shall give three reasons for preferring the imagination theory of delusion to the hallucination theory. First, there is nothing *irrational* about forming false beliefs on the basis of illusions and hallucinations: if it really perceptually seems to you as if there is someone threatening in front of you, then it is rational to believe that there is—even if in fact your perception is mistaken. But the delusional subject has something *wrong* with the way he forms beliefs. He is irrational; and his irrationality consists in letting his beliefs be driven by what is merely imaginary, since images are the wrong *kind* of thing to base beliefs upon. The hallucination theory makes the delusional believer too *sane* when it comes to how he forms his beliefs; the pathology is shifted onto merely malfunctioning senses. The massively false beliefs of the brain in a vat are not symptoms of insane irrationality, but the false beliefs of the deluded schizophrenic are paradigmatically irrational. And it is certainly irrational to give assent to one's own imaginings.

Second, hallucinations proper are occlusive, so that the deluded subject ought to be suffering from perceptual failures—partial blindness, partial deafness. While undergoing an auditory hallucination, say, he ought to be unable to hear properly what is going on around him; there should be perceptual interference effects. But this seems to be empirically false: his hearing is unimpaired by the voices in his head; these voices never drown out the sounds around him. This is consistent with the image theory, since auditory images can coexist with auditory percepts. Such images do not occur in the "auditory field" of the subject but rather belong in the space of imagination. Nor does the subject incline his head in the direction of the supposed voice, listening to catch its intonations more clearly; he simply hears the voice as he would an auditory image. What is special is that he gives credence to this image—he lets it shape his beliefs. The subject hears voices "in his head," which is not the same as erroneously hearing them with his ears. He thus believes what he merely imagines.

Third, there is a subtle difference of affective tone in the case of the deluded subject: his emotions are not exactly what they would be if he were really seeing and hearing what he merely imagines. The case here is analogous to that of the dreamer: the fear of a dreamed-of tiger is not quite the same as fear of a perceived tiger; there is always a hint of "inauthenticity" in the accompanying emotion.[4] The same seems to be true of the deluded subject: his paranoia, say, is never quite as real as that of someone who really is being persecuted and knows this in the ordinary way. The source of the belief in the imagination is somehow registered in his mind, thus modifying the force of the correlated emotions. Hence there is always something a touch melodramatic in the delusional subject's errant belief system and associated emotions—despite the reality of his suffering. Just as with the dream, it is hard to characterize this difference precisely, but one knows it when one sees it. It is not that the emotion is necessarily less intense, but it is more . . . fantastic—more a creature of the imagination. It sometimes seems like a *game* the patient is playing with himself, an internally enacted drama (we sometimes speak of "psychodrama" here), a flight away from the real world and into a fictional world. But if the delusional state of mind were percept-driven, then there would be no differences of these kinds.

An author who gets all this right is Karl Jaspers in *General Psychopathology*—not surprisingly, since he was an acute phenomenologist, well attuned to the distinctions among mental states. Jaspers identifies a category of what he labels "pseudohallucinations," remarking that these "were for a long time confused with hallucinations. Looked at closely these proved to be not really perceptions but a special kind of imagery."[5] He goes on to note, correctly in my view, that the pseudohallucinations, though powerful, are apprehended by the inner eye and are not presented as within the visual field, "nor do they possess the reality of perception."[6] Instead, "pseudohallucinations lack concrete reality and appear in inner subjective space."[7] Jaspers has clearly distinguished percepts from images earlier, and so is able to make room for the idea of a mental state that functions partly like a hallucination—in that it generates belief—but is nevertheless an image. Contemporary authors are more apt to employ a very vaguely delineated concept of hallucination—as something like "sensory state that induces belief"—and hence are unable to make the distinction that Jaspers rightly perceives. Here is an area in which phenomenology abetted by analytic philosophy of mind can clarify some of the phenomena dealt with by psychiatry and psychopathology.[8]

And this matters practically, because we obviously need to know *what* has gone wrong in the mind of the delusional subject—precisely what psychic structures are malfunctioning. Only then can we decide what the best cure might be. Does the patient have a perceptual defect or a defect of the imagination? In practice, I think, the former option is seldom taken seriously, since the senses of the patient appear to be functioning normally; but the usual description of the case locates the problem in defective perception—in the occurrence of hallucinations. It would serve clarity to reserve the term "hallucination" only for perceptual malfunctions and substitute some other term for the odd states of the deluded subject—"pseudohallucination" or "belief-producing image."

The image-based conception of delusion raises an obvious question: Who or what is controlling the images? Are they subject to the patient's will? If they are, then he is presumably unaware of this; for, if he were consciously and intentionally willing his images, then he would know that this is how they arise. But then, how could he believe them and generate the associated emotions? He cannot simultaneously consciously manipulate his images and also believe that they tell him how things objectively are. This would require bad faith and confusion on a colossal scale. I think it is more plausible to suppose that his psychological state resembles that of the dreamer, in that he has undergone a "psychic split." That is, an unconscious component of his mind is controlling the course of his imagery, so that it appears to come to him unwilled; hence his readiness to believe it. Perhaps, indeed, as with dreams, there is a hypnotic aspect to his state of mind: his suggestibility has been increased by the unconscious agent that is generating the images. This would certainly explain his degree of conviction; the imagery has an especially tight grip over his beliefs and emotions. In any case, it seems likely that the causation of the images does not lie in the patient's conscious will. The causation of imagery has gone underground in madness, and the belief system is accordingly seduced and manipulated. It is as if the mind has become unconsciously commandeered by the imagination, as it is in dreams, and perception retreats to a subordinate role—even overridden by the imagination in the production of beliefs.

This picture of what is going on admits of empirical verification. We could test for any evidence of perceptual occlusion. We could test for the stronger presence of mental imagery in the case of the insane. We could determine whether schizophrenics have trouble with image control: Can they form and banish images as easily as sane people? Are they subject to a lot of unbidden imagery? Can they generally tell what is an image and what is not? My guess is that in tasks of ordinary controlled image formation they will not perform as well as sane people, thus confirming the idea that it is their imagination system that has gone awry. So far as I know, such investigations have not been undertaken, possibly because of lack of clarity about the percept/image distinction. It would be interesting, too, to test the capacity for imaginative seeing and hearing: is this as controllable for the insane as for the sane? What about image rotation and scanning tasks? Might the total imagination system be divided into dissociable modules, some of which remain functionally intact while others have failed?

The general conceptual apparatus I have proposed suggests the following investigation: look to see whether the various motor abnormalities that exist have counterparts in the realm of the imagination. Compulsions, tics, spasms, stereotyped behaviors, and paralysis: do these have parallels with respect to the imagination? In what specific ways can imagination become decoupled from the will? Is there a Tourette's syndrome of the imagination—an uncontrollable cascade of imagery, which may be both disturbing and sometimes welcome? Can the imagination cease to be active, as the body can in paralysis? As there can be repetitive tics of the body, can there also be tics of the mind—sudden volleys of imagery that come and go for no apparent reason? The body is subject to the will, obviously, and it can suffer many different sorts of breakdown of voluntary control; if the imagination is also, then it too should exhibit comparable varieties of breakdown. The imagination should be as prone to conative upset as the body, and there ought to be many varieties of imaginative pathology.

My aim in this chapter has been to suggest a conceptual structure with which to approach such questions. Empirical research needs to be informed by this structure. The essential point, again, is to keep in mind a clear distinction between percepts and images. Once this is done, delusion emerges as a special case of imagination-driven belief, analogous to dreaming; no sensory illusion need be postulated. Madness is the imagination gone awry. Obviously, this confirms the often remarked kinship between dreaming and madness.[9]

The Imagination of the Child

Very little is scientifically known about the phenomenology of the infant mind: about what it is like to be a baby. But we can at least venture some speculations. Presumably percepts (better: sensations) abound, however unarticulated they may be. These will no doubt have the characteristics of percepts that I listed in Chapter 1; particularly, they will not be subject to the will. When images make their appearance is a matter of guesswork in the current state of knowledge, but I think we can assume that they initially enter the mind in the form of memory images, prompted by earlier percepts. It is highly doubtful that the infant recognizes these images *as* images—doubtful that she *judges* them to be what they are. They simply commingle with percepts in the phenomenological soup, not yet differentiated out. For the infant, images and percepts blur together.

From this initial state, three achievements are necessary for the image system to attain maturity: (1) images must come under voluntary control, (2) they must enter into the correct relationship with belief, and (3) they must be conceptually differentiated from percepts. The child must make images subject to her will, she must know not to believe them, and she must be able to tell when she is having one. These three achievements constitute the "output" of the maturation process. In all probability there will be a "critical period" during which this process must occur—just as there is a critical period for language learning. The process might of course be disrupted, in which case there may be a failure to achieve conditions 1–3, but normally the process proceeds without a hitch; we become masters of our imagination.

How do these three accomplishments occur? Allow me to speculate: my hypothesis is that control comes first, then correct belief alignment, then conceptual differentiation. I offer this as a piece of rational reconstruction; it would be extremely hard to verify empirically. We may suppose that at some stage the child discovers that some of its sensory contents can be manipulated at will and some may not—much as some of its bodily movements may be willed and some may not. Perhaps this is a matter of trial and error, or perhaps it is the unfolding of an innate program. In any case, a deep distinction in the sensory states that besiege the child's consciousness is recognized. This reflects the different nature of their causation, among other things. In the first instance we may assume that memory images are selected out as controllable, while their perceptual originals are not. Once this is appreciated, the question of what to believe becomes tractable: you can believe the involuntary percepts but not the voluntary images. Perhaps this becomes evident because of the different effects on action that the respective beliefs produce: in the case of percepts, the belief works out well; in the case of images, it leads to unsuccessful action (there is no use believing that mother is present when you are only remembering her via a memory image). This transition may not be a matter of ceasing to believe what is merely imagined; it could rather be commencing to believe what the percepts indicate.[1] What matters is that beliefs get correctly aligned with the perceptual and imaginative faculties. Subjection to the will, I conjecture, is the cue that guides this alignment.

The next stage is coming to possess and apply the concept of imagination. This emerges via the idea of what can and cannot be believed: the concept of imagination corresponds to the notion of a sensory state that should not be believed; the concept of perception corresponds to one that can and should be. Thus the concept of reality is part of what is involved in grasping the concept of the merely imaginary: it is what is *not* real. The child treats an experience as a percept, by contrast, just when she acknowledges that it constitutes a good ground for belief. The concept of imagination thus has roots in two prior concepts: the concept of what can (and cannot) be willed, and the concept of what can (and cannot) be believed. The child undergoes a volitional maturation in which the domain of the will is gradually established and delineated, and awareness of this is what generates the concept of imagination. Other marks of the imaginary follow, but I conjecture that the connection to volition is the initial distinguishing feature: an image is *(inter alia)* a sensory representation that can be willed.[2]

Children are notoriously susceptible to the products of their imagination. They are often afraid of what they have merely imagined. In this they resemble both the dreamer and the delusional adult. Their beliefs are still tethered partially to their imagination. It is not that they *hallucinate* in the dark, and then endorse their hallucinations. Rather, they form images and let their beliefs and emotions be shaped by these. There is nothing amiss with their senses, and their fancies don't occlude their perception of the world. It is just that they cannot help believing what their imagination conjures up. They are especially prone to this error in the dark, probably because their senses offer no substantial input to compete with their imagination; their consciousness becomes crowded with images, and there are only feeble percepts to divert belief. The dream, then, is a kind of nightly regression to childhood in terms of the psychological configuration involved; and insanity is also regressive in this way.[3] It is as if imagination naturally pulls belief toward it, despite its unsuitability as a basis for belief, and only the forces of maturity, sanity, and daylight can keep them apart. (Were our distant ancestors powerfully prone to form their beliefs about the world according to what their imagination cooked up?)

Dreaming, childhood, insanity, and superstition thus form a natural family: imagination-driven belief.

How might we test for possession of the concept of imagination in the child? Psychologists have devised the so-called "false belief" test, designed to reveal when a child has acquired the concept of belief.[4] Briefly, it runs as follows: One child, the subject, is shown two boxes into one of which a marble is placed. This is done in front of another child, who is then asked to leave the room. While this child is out, the marble is switched to the other box in plain sight of the subject child. The other child returns, and the subject is asked where the child who did not witness the switch believes the marble is. Before a certain age, around three, the subject is apt to say that the other child believes the marble is in the box it is *actually* in, after the switch, and not the box it *was* in before the other child left the room—despite the fact that the other child has no reason to believe that any switch has occurred. The subject child attributes to the other child the belief that *he* has and is unable to entertain the idea that the other child has a false (though justified) belief. Thus the subject child does not yet have the concept of belief, which admits of the possibility of falsehood; he doesn't yet grasp that people can differ in the beliefs they hold. In this way, then, we can test for whether the concept of belief has been grasped and understood.

I want to suggest a similar kind of test for possession of the concept of imagination. Again, there are two children, one of them the subject; the other one is told to form an image of something that is not the case ("Picture in your mind your father with a mustache"), with the subject observing. The subject is then asked what the other child believes about the object imagined ("Does he believe his father has a mustache?"). If the subject thinks that the other child believes what he has merely imagined, then he has failed to grasp that images don't warrant belief and hasn't cottoned onto the concept of imagination yet: he hasn't distinguished percepts from images. The general idea is to determine whether the child understands that images are not good evidence for truth. So we might also compare the subject child's judgments about the other child's beliefs in conditions of both perception and imagination: does he understand that if the other child *sees* something, then he has a right to believe it, but not if he merely imagines it? Of course, the child has to grasp enough of the concept of imagination in order to understand what is being asked of him—namely, whether the other child's image leads to belief. But I would predict that children of a certain age will be able to follow the instructions and yet fail to grasp that images don't warrant belief. In any case, the question is obviously an empirical one. It should be possible, therefore, to ascertain whether a child has grasped this essential feature of imagination and how it differs from perception.[5]

Let us suppose that my speculations are on the right lines: that the child learns, through his different volitional relation to images and percepts, that belief attaches rightly to one and not to the other. What might disturb or arrest this psychological progression? What might interfere with normal image/percept differentiation? And what might the result of such interference be? Suppose the child's environment is made intolerable, so that the perceived world is one in which the child has no desire to live. This may be brought about in many ways: intentional abuse, abject poverty, conditions of war. All that is necessary is a range of perceptual stimuli that the child does not *want* to believe—that it is intolerable for the child to accept. I would think that severe parental abuse would be high on this list of unwanted realities. Then imagination—an imaginary world—might well seem preferable, more in conformity with the child's wishes. Wouldn't it be wonderful if *that* world were the real one? We thus have a potent basis for aligning belief with imagination, not perception; it is just so much easier on the emotions to believe what is imagined instead of what is perceived. If these conditions occur during the critical period for aligning belief with perception, they might well disrupt that development, and the child will remain confused about the difference between reality and imagination. He may well become "fixated" on his imagination, unable to detach his beliefs from the wished-for imaginary world and attach them to the perceived real world. A kind of "reality inversion" occurs.[6] We have all heard about unhappy children who choose to live in their imaginary world instead of the intolerable real world around them; my suggestion is that in extreme cases the belief system becomes permanently attached to imagination and never makes the step to perception. In essence, the imaginary world takes on the status of the real world, so far as the child's beliefs are concerned, and the crucial distinction between percept and image is never made. It may therefore take a lot of agreeable perceptual experiences to wean the child from this mental configuration, and perhaps in some cases it will be impossible to do so.

The results of such attachment to the imagination are easy to predict: the delusions of the insane. Just as the deluded adult lets his beliefs be shaped by his imagination, with perception correspondingly demoted, so the child may have his beliefs determined by the preferred imaginary world; in other words, the seeds of insanity may be sown by the process of interference I have described. Put simply, a causal factor in generating delusional personality may be intolerable childhood experience—hardly a novel insight on my part. What I have done is to locate this familiar theme against a conceptual and theoretical background—specifying the mental architecture, as they say. To investigate the matter further, we would need to know when the critical period occurs and what experiences interfere most profoundly with it. My hypothesis is that it occurs pretty early, before the age of three, and that it is primarily family trauma that has the deepest effect. Fear is the most likely cause of withdrawal from the perceived world, abetted by the desperate expedient of shifting belief from percept to image. The result will resemble living in a dream, except that there is the constant collision with the world of sense experience—which only adds to the confusion. Delusional tendencies are the result of an imagination that has not grown up—one that still functions as it does in dreams.

I shall leave these speculations with yet another, which I hope will not be thought frivolous. During adolescence the fear so often associated with the child's imagination seems to retreat considerably; darkness is no longer an occasion for wild and terrible fancies. Why is this? Well, a contemporaneous development is the onset of puberty and its psychological expression—specifically, sexual desire and the fantasies it generates. I trust it will surprise no one if I suggest that the imagination becomes dominated by these sexual images at this time, crowding out those earlier images of fear. The focus shifts from one kind of image to another, at the behest of a new type of desire. There are now new things to occupy the fevered imagination in the dark. So we have sex to thank for freeing our imagination from its childish fears.[7]

Cognitive Imagination

I have so far been discussing mental imagery—a type of sensory content of consciousness. The linguistic form of an ascription of imagery is "X imagines Y," which has the form of a two-place predicate (like "X sees Y"). I now want to discuss another use of the concept of imagination, the kind that is followed by a "that" clause: "X imagines that p." This exercise of imagination falls into the same family as other propositional attitudes, such as belief; it takes a propositional object. I shall call this "cognitive imagination." It takes conceptual constituents, not sensory ones. Roughly speaking, it is to imagery proper what believing is to perception—a conceptual capacity that may be related to sensory contents but is not reducible to such contents. Cognitive imagination is a type of *thought,* in the broadest sense. If I imagine that I am in Paris, I entertain a thought—the thought that I am in Paris. This may or may not be accompanied by imagery proper; in any case, it is a conceptual act, with all the marks thereof.

To see the distinction between sensory and cognitive imagination, consider Descartes's example of the chiliogon.[1] Descartes used this example to show that understanding is not the same as imagination, since one can conceive of a thousand-sided figure but one cannot form an image of one. I think he is right in the substance of his point but wrong in his formulation of what it shows: what it really shows is that imagery is not the same as imagining-that. I can imagine *that* there is a chiliogon in the next room; I just cannot form an image of one (that is distinct from my image of a 1,001-sided figure). I can combine the concepts in question and adopt the attitude of imagination toward the resulting propositional content; I just cannot make my *image* that fine-grained (it is a question whether my percept could be that fine-grained too). The lesson is that cognitive imagination can outstrip sensory imagination in its representational content; it is not that imagination cannot encompass such concepts, *pace* Descartes. I can also imagine that I am seeing something red now, but it is unclear that I can form an image of an experience of red, as opposed to what such an experience is of; images seem necessarily of perceptible objects. I can imagine that democracy will triumph over tyranny, but what would it be to form an *image* of democracy triumphing over tyranny? Mental states and abstractions are resistant to representation by means of images, yet they can readily feature in the contents of propositional imagining.

Once this distinction is appreciated, it becomes a question why we use the word "imagination" in such an inclusive way: Is it ambiguous between sensory and cognitive imagination? Does it just lump together unrelated mental operations? This is a reasonable question, but I think it has an answer—namely, the two types of imagination employ different *elements* but involve the same *faculty*. Sensory imagination employs sensory elements, much as perception does—though, as we have extensively seen, these elements must not be conflated.[2] Cognitive imagination employs conceptual elements, much as thinking does: these elements are not intrinsically modality-specific, and combine to form propositional contents. What is in common is the general faculty that works on these elements—the imagination. It is essentially a creative combinatorial faculty that differs from perception and from belief (as we shall see more fully in a moment). My point is just that the *same* faculty may operate on distinct types of elements; the identity consists in the same type of operation being performed by a structurally uniform faculty.[3] As we shall see, cognitive imagination displays several points of similarity to sensory imagination. So the two types of imagination are correctly so called.

Let us first satisfy ourselves that imagining-that is not merely a type of belief. The idea that it might be is analogous to the Humean doctrine that images are a type of percept: as images are said to be faint percepts, so imaginings may be said to be faint beliefs. Thus, to imagine that I am in Paris is to hesitantly or weakly believe that I am in Paris. The thought here is that belief comes in degrees, from mere suspicion to overwhelming conviction, and that imagining is just low-grade belief—belief with low subjective probability or some such. It is easy to see that this suggestion is mistaken. The reason is simple: I can imagine that p without having any tendency whatever to believe that p. I know perfectly well that I am not in Paris, and I have no evidence that favors such a hypothesis; but this does not stop me one whit from *imagining* that I am in Paris. This is no more impossible than knowing I am not a famous movie star and *wishing* I were; indeed, my so wishing might well involve imagining that it is so. I can even imagine that I do not exist, while being perfectly convinced for Cartesian reasons that I definitely *do* exist. So imagining is clearly not a case of faintly believing.

But might it be the belief that the imagined state of affairs is *possible?* This sounds better, but it is still wrong. The alleged analysis stipulates a necessary condition for imagining that it does not have, since I can imagine that p and be *neutral* on the question of the possibility of p. Perhaps I can imagine only what is possible, but I do not have to *assent* to the proposition that it is possible in order to imagine it. Can I not imagine something and falsely believe that it is impossible? The essential point is that I often imagine all sorts of things without giving a thought to whether they are possible, or in what sense they are possible. In dreams I may imagine that I am flying, but I do not concern myself with the modal question of whether what I am imagining is really possible. When I am imagining, I am not necessarily conducting a modal investigation or giving expression to my modal beliefs. The attitude of imagining a possibility is not the same as the attitude of believing that it *is* a possibility—which is why I may not care whether what I am imagining is possible or not. I might even be a skeptic about modal categories and refrain from ever employing them. That won't stop me from imagining things. Believing that something is possible might *result* from an act of imagining, but it is not what that act *consists in*.

Imagining may be compared with uttering a sentence, as distinct from asserting it.[4] If I simply utter a sentence, say, in the course of practicing my pronunciation, I represent a state of affairs—the one expressed by the sentence—but I don't thereby assert that the state of affairs is possible. I am modally neutral on this question *qua* speaker. By merely uttering the sentence I express no modal commitments. Nor, of course, do I hesitantly or weakly assert what the sentence says. I merely represent the possibility without asserting that it *is* a possibility. In the same way, if I imagine a possibility, I do not thereby believe that it *is* a possibility. Entertaining a thought is not taking a stand on its modal status.

These points show that imagining cannot be analyzed in terms of belief; the verb "imagine" connotes a distinct type of attitude altogether. I now want to bring out some further dissimilarities to belief, which will underline the *sui generis* status of the attitude of imagining-that and also indicate some parallels with imagery proper.

First, imagining that p is an action, while believing that p is not. More exactly, imagining is subject to the will, while believing is not. You may undertake to entertain the possibility that p, succeed in this endeavor, persist for a period of time, and then decide to desist. You can try to imagine something and fail. You can expend a lot of effort in imagining something. You can compulsively imagine certain things. The case is just like forming an image in this respect. But, notoriously, you cannot decide to believe—any more than you can decide to see. Belief is passive, not within the domain of the will.[5] Belief is a commitment to truth, and the truth cannot be willed into being. But imagining is not a commitment to truth, even possible truth, so there is no obstacle to willing it; imagining something is simply contemplating it, holding it before the mind. To decide to imagine something is no more difficult than deciding to read something—irrespective of the truth-value of what you read. Entertaining a thought is voluntary, believing is not; the conceptual contents may coincide, but the attitudes are very different. So, in this respect, imagining-that contrasts with belief in the way that forming an image contrasts with perception.

A connected point is that imagining is "evidence-indifferent," while belief is not. That there is strong evidence against a proposition is no bar to imagining that it is true, since I am not, *qua* imaginer, in the business of conducting an investigation of how the world is. But evidence against a proposition is obviously germane to whether I should believe it. When I am in the business of investigating the world, I adopt an attitude of evidential sensitivity, and my beliefs are formed accordingly; but not so when I am merely imagining. Here I am indifferent to how things actually are. This parallels the earlier notion (discussed in Chapter 1) of the "observational attitude," which is present in perception but not in the forming of images. Perception and belief purport to get things right, so they involve sensitivity to evidence; but forming images and imagining-that do not purport to depict how things really are. Thus one needs reasons for belief, but reasons are not necessary for imagination. I can imagine that p and have no reasons whatever in favor of p—and I cannot be accused of irrationality either.

Third, there is a parallel to occlusion, or the lack of it. Images do not preclude percepts; the two can coexist in consciousness. Similarly, imaginings do not preclude beliefs: I can easily imagine that p while believing that not-p. Nothing in what I imagine precludes my believing anything; the two are not in competition. Of course, beliefs compete with other beliefs; they are "occlusive." But, as we have seen, imagining is not a form of belief. If it were, then imagining that p would interfere with believing that not-p, even if the alleged imaginative belief were merely faint or hesitant. There seems, however, no analogue to Wittgenstein's point that I cannot form a visual image of an object that I am currently looking at. For it does seem possible for me to believe that p *and* to imagine that p. Suppose I believe that it is raining outside, though I have no direct perception of this: the curtains are closed, et cetera. I can still surely imagine that it is raining: I might simply form a mental image of rain outside, and this will be sufficient in the circumstances to have imagined *that* it is raining. Of course, it will be conversationally misleading to say "I am imagining that it is raining" when I know full well that it is—since my utterance will give the impression that I am in doubt or even disbelieve that it is raining. But I take it this is just a conversational implicature and does not show that it is *false* that I am imagining it. Can I imagine that I am a philosopher? Sure, even though I know I am. It might be misleading to say "I imagine that I'm a philosopher" to someone who doesn't know that I know I am, but I don't think it would be false. So believing that p and imagining that p are logically consistent.[6]

Fourth, entertaining is more closely tied to attending than belief is. You can have many beliefs you are not currently paying attention to; the beliefs are "dispositional" and do not require to be present to consciousness at all times, still less at the focus of attention. But imaginings seem different: they do require an act of attention. This is why you can have many beliefs simultaneously, but there are definite limits on your ability to entertain different things at the same time. You have to pay attention to what you are imagining in order to imagine it, but you don't have to pay attention to the content of your beliefs in order to have them.[7] It might well be true that you can have a *disposition* to imagine something that doesn't require an act of attention, but such a disposition is not itself a case of imagining; while in the case of belief, a disposition to accept something in the attentive mode *is* a belief. Imaginings, in short, are attention-dependent, but beliefs are not.

Thus imagining-that differs in many ways from belief; it belongs to another mental category altogether. I would say that the general category of *thinking* has two species—believing and entertaining—just as I said earlier that the general category of seeing has two species—perceptual seeing and mental seeing.[8] Neither of these species should be regarded as conceptually basic with respect to the other; so, in particular, we should not suppose that (occurrent) believing is the basic form of thinking and entertaining is derivative or secondary. If anything, it is the other way about, as we shall shortly see. Belief is not the paradigm propositional attitude, with imagining as its pale copy; rather, both form the twin pillars of cognitive life. Imagining and believing are *alike* in certain respects (particularly with regard to their conceptual ingredients), but they are not to be assimilated—just as images and percepts are alike in certain respects but are not to be assimilated. Images and imaginings are not the poor relatives of percepts and beliefs; they have their own distinctive characteristics and place in the mind.

The distinctness of imagination and belief does not mean that the two can never combine. Is there an analogue here for imaginative sensing, in which percept and image combine? Imagination can affect the way things look; can it also insert itself into the content of belief? I think it can—in the phenomenon of *metaphorical belief*. Suppose I employ a simile to express my belief: I say that the sky is like the ocean. What I have done is imagine the sky *as* the ocean, and thus associate the concept of the ocean with the concept of the sky. I think of the sky under an imaginative aspect—rather as I can see an object under an imaginative aspect. The content of my belief thus combines a literal component, corresponding to the concept *sky,* and also an imposed imaginative component, corresponding to the concept *ocean.* If I then say "The sky is an ocean," speaking metaphorically, I condense these two components into one, and I give expression to a metaphorical belief content. My imagination has penetrated my belief, so to speak—as my mental imagery can penetrate my perceptions in cases of seeing-as. And isn't this mental operation essentially voluntary? I can't help believing that the sky is vast and blue, but to think of it metaphorically as oceanic seems a matter of decision; we do *choose* our metaphors, after all. I might decide that this is a banal metaphor—the sky as ocean—and opt to delete it from my belief content; perhaps instead I decide to compare the sky to a desert. It's not as if the facts dictate one metaphor rather than the other; the metaphor comes from my own free creativity. It is my *interpretation* of the facts. It is how I choose to imagine the (imposed) facts. Not surprisingly, given this subjection to the will, metaphorical beliefs are not evidence-sensitive: there is no evidence I might come across that will favor one metaphor over the other. I do not, in forming a metaphorical belief, stand ready to adjust my description in the light of further evidence; for I am not making a claim about how things objectively are. The poet is not in the business of making refutable assertions about objective reality when she offers us a metaphorical description. It would be silly for someone to come along and announce that it has just been discovered that the sky is *not* like a desert. The poet could reasonably retort, "Well, it is *to me*." Metaphor making is not an attempt to get something objectively there right—though of course metaphors can be more or less apt, more or less evocative, and so on. This is just what we would expect, given the role of the imagination in generating them. So metaphorical belief parallels imaginative seeing in several respects. It is the cognitive imagination fusing with belief, as the sensory imagination can fuse with perception in cases of seeing-as.[9]

I have said that imagining is not a type of belief, and neither is belief a type of imagining. But these failures of equivalence do not imply that imagination is not somehow *involved* in belief—embedded in it, presupposed by it. So how are the two related? Here is one very obvious point: you can imagine a state of affairs before you come to believe that it obtains. You might conjure up a hypothesis by means of imagination, and subsequently you verify that the hypothesis is true—thus coming to believe what you earlier merely imagined. You entertain a possibility, and later come to believe that it is actualized. Question: do you *stop* entertaining the possibility once you believe it to be actualized, or do you persist with your entertaining? Does belief extinguish imagination, or does it add to it? If the latter, then belief is imagination plus something—rather as knowledge is belief plus something. I shall argue for this position. Of course, there are conversational implicatures to contend with: you won't *say* "I imagine that p" if you actually believe that p, in normal circumstances—rather as you won't say you believe that p when you are well aware that you know that p.[10] That would be to assert the weaker thing when the stronger thing is known to be true, and hence suggest that the stronger thing isn't true. The real question is whether the initial mental state of imagining survives the arrival of the new state of believing: do you cease to entertain a hypothesis when you come to believe it? Suppose at a still later time you cease to believe the hypothesis, though you persist in entertaining it. Do you then begin a new phase of entertaining that had been interrupted by belief? I think this is implausible. Just as I don't stop believing when I start knowing (say, by acquiring a good justification), so I don't stop entertaining when I start believing. Believing is really entertaining a thought plus assenting to it; so there is a constant state of entertaining that is supplemented by internal assent.[11] When I believe that p, I (1) contemplate the possibility that p and (2) take this possibility to be actual. So hypothesis confirmation is verification of an imagined possibility, where the act of imagining does not stop.

We have to be a bit careful in formulating this claim correctly. It is not that at any time at which you have a belief you are actually entertaining its associated possibility, since belief is dispositional and entertaining is occurrent (as I noted earlier); rather, you are *disposed* to entertain what you believe at any time that you believe it. Put differently, whenever you occurrently believe that p, you are actually entertaining the possibility that p—that is, employing your cognitive imagination in representing that state of affairs. Imagination is what brings a possibility to mind; belief simply tags it as actual. You *represent* the possibility by means of your imaginative faculty, and then belief consists in accepting what is thus represented. I prefer this account of the matter to the view that belief extinguishes entertaining, because there is a mental representation of a possibility both in the merely imagined phase and in the belief phase—and the right name for this is "entertaining/imagining." Also, there is no *experience* of losing a mental state when an imagined hypothesis is confirmed; rather, something is added to what was there before. Just as the adding of an object to a hallucination, thereby producing a veridical perception, does not extinguish the original experience but supplements it, so adding confirmation to imagining, thereby producing belief, does not extinguish imagining. In short, I favor a *conjunctive* analysis of these concepts.[12] In a sense, then, the propositional attitude of imagining is more fundamental than the propositional attitude of believing, since the latter presupposes the former as a necessary condition (but not conversely).

I have been speaking of imagination as the representation of possibility, and of course this is a very familiar idea: imagination is the faculty that puts us in touch with the non-actual. I want to make just two brief observations about this. First, there is an analogy here with imagery: the image presents its object as absent, while perception presents it as present; imagination deals with the merely possible, while knowledge deals with the actual. To be presented as present is to be presented as actual; to be presented as absent—that is, neutrally with respect to location and existence—is to move away from the actual. The image frees itself from the constraints of location and reality; its object is placed in a kind of limbo—not represented as a real denizen of objective space. Cognitive imagination takes us to alternative worlds, but the image was already detaching its objects from the constraints of reality. The image was already liberating the mind from the domination of perception. So there is a kind of continuity between sensory and cognitive imagination with respect to the non-actual: cognitive imagination continues and extends what the humble image had already initiated—a flight from the world of perceived reality.[13]

Second, we need to be clear about the connection between imagination and modal knowledge or belief. I don't mean the question of whether imagination can give rise to reliable modal knowledge; I mean the question of what the relationship is *when* it gives rise to modal knowledge. It is not, I think, that imagination *expresses* our modal knowledge, or is *identical* with it. Rather, imagination is the *means* by which we acquire modal knowledge; it functions to supply *reasons* for modal belief. So the relationship is inferential, not constitutive. I say this partly because of a point I made earlier, namely that imagination itself is modally neutral; you can imagine something and take no stand on its modal status. Imagining that p is not, constitutively, believing that p is possible. If you believe that p is possible as a result of imagining that p, then this is an inferential step, a substantive epistemic move. The relationship between imagination and modal belief is therefore not direct but mediated—and complex. I have no intention of trying to address this large question here; I wish only to point out that distinguishing the concept of imagination from that of modal belief leaves the question of their connection open. The way I would look at it is that modal beliefs are best seen as based on inferences to the best explanation with respect to acts of imagination—not deductions. If you find that you can consistently imagine something, and you are trying to figure out what modal beliefs to hold, then you can explain your successful imaginings by the assumption that the thing in question is indeed possible. I think, in fact, that modal belief relates to imagination in very much the way that ordinary knowledge relates to perception. Percepts don't *entail* beliefs about the external world, but they can function as data in an inference to the best explanation. Your epistemic relation to your imaginings is similar: they can function as data that a system of modal belief attempts to explain.[14] But with that brief statement I shall leave the vexed topic of how modal beliefs are rationally generated.

Negation

In this short chapter I want to bring out the especially intimate relation between the concept of negation and imagination. Negation enters our thoughts not by means of perception but by means of imagination. This has a bearing on the nature of belief formation and the faculties implicated in logical reasoning.

Suppose I observe that the grass is green and thereby come to know this. I might then go on to entertain the possibility that the grass is *not* green: I might start to doubt my senses, or I might just be considering other possible worlds. This employment of the concept of negation marks my departure from the actual—from the information supplied by my senses. And in so doing it brings the imagination into play: I imagine the state of affairs in which grass is not green. Negating what I perceive is how I enter the realm of the merely possible: I observe one thing and then use my imagination to represent its opposite, with negation as my tool. Negation is not itself a possible perceptual content: I cannot *see* that something is *not* so, in the way that I can that something is green.[1] The not-greenness of sand is not a perceptible property of sand. When I look at sand and judge that it is not green, I make an inference from what I see—namely that sand is yellow. I don't have a primitive experience of the not-greenness of sand. There is no such thing as having an experience *as of* negation; negation is a concept of thought, not perception. Animals that perceive but don't think have no acquaintance with the concept of negation. What I am saying is that when we use negation to generate an alternative to what we perceive, we necessarily employ imagination, because we have to represent what is merely possible. Our thoughts of the non-actual are imaginative thoughts, exercises of the cognitive imagination. The role of negation in generating thoughts of the non-actual is an achievement of the imagination. So the occurrence of negation in reasoning or belief formation is always a sign of the operation of the imagination—that is, of the entertaining of thoughts (as opposed to the perception of facts). Let me illustrate how this works.

I believe that grass is green; this means that I reject the claim that it is not green. To reject that claim, I have to represent the *possibility* that grass is not green—only to deny that it obtains. Belief formation is a matter of the rejection of alternatives, but this rejection has to bring with it the representation of these alternatives— which means that they have to be entertained. When I reject the proposition that not-p, I have at least to *entertain* that proposition. If I deny that grass is blue in the process of affirming that it is green, then I do at least contemplate the state of affairs in which grass is blue—which means that I imaginatively represent that state of affairs. Belief is selection from among imagined possibilities: when I believe that grass is green, I reject the alternative possibilities that my imagination presents to me. I hold that those possibilities are *not* so, thus employing my imagination in the very act of rejection. Accepting one proposition is rejecting its negation, so that acceptance presupposes the entertaining of the negation. The imagination represents the entire logical space, and the belief system narrows this down. I entertain many possibilities, but I believe only a subset of these. I can imagine grass having many colors, but my belief system accepts only one.

If this is right, then imagination enters belief formation at two points: first, in the representation of what is believed (which I argued in the previous chapter); second, in the representation of the *negation* of what is believed. If belief formation is selection from alternatives, then the alternatives need to be represented, and imagination is the faculty for the job. In believing that p, you imagine that p *and also* imagine that not-p. So imagination is deeply embedded in belief; it is the *sine qua non* of belief. Frank Ramsey said that a belief is "a map by which we steer."[2] I am saying that the terrain we steer through is vouchsafed to us by the imagination, since it tells us all the ways the world *might* be.

It could be objected that not all belief formation involves the rejection of alternatives. Isn't simple perceptual belief a counterexample—believing what strikes the senses without considering any alternatives? I am prepared to concede that some beliefs can be formed in this way (I don't want to quibble about the word "believe"); what I am saying is that *rational, reflective* belief is selection from imagined alternatives. In cases in which I am reasoning about what to believe and have set the options out, *this* will involve the use of imagination to represent the options. My point is that imagination is crucially implicated in this kind of selective belief formation; it is not some separate faculty that has nothing directly to do with the serious business of believing things. Imagination does not exist just for purposes of fancy and distraction; it is bound up with the very essence of rational, reflective belief formation—and hence with arriving at knowledge of the world. In science, it is often said, we imagine a hypothesis and then try to confirm it; I am saying that this is the general case with belief formation—and we *also* imagine alternatives to the hypothesis (even if just the simple negation). Imagination, negation, possibility, and belief are all interconnected notions.[3]

It is this that animals generally lack, though some may be capable of it. Animals don't generally have the ability to reject the negations of what they believe; they don't select from among imagined alternatives, using the concept of negation to do so. There is thus a large difference between a creature whose beliefs are formed in this way and one whose beliefs (or "beliefs") are simply responses to stimuli. Reflective belief is embedded in a sophisticated set of capacities involving imagination and the representation of negation. It is not the mere trace of a perceptual stimulus as it strikes the sensorium, nor even the isolated assent to some internal sentence. The interesting question is not whether animals have beliefs but what *kinds* of beliefs they have; and I suspect that, generally speaking, they lack the kind that are embedded in a matrix of imagination.

The bearing of this conception of belief on logical reasoning is clear: imagination must be integrally employed in such reasoning. In logic we are always asking what would follow upon a certain supposition—but this is precisely to contemplate a possibility and hence to employ the imagination. The thought "What if?" always presupposes a shift to the merely possible and hence an exercise of imagination. Suppose such-and-such were so: what would follow? This very suppositional act brings in the imaginative faculty. (Frege put an assertion sign before the propositions that were taken to be asserted; he might have put an imagination sign before all the others.) The idea that the validity of an argument does not require the truth of the premises involves thinking of the premises as mere possibilities—things to entertain, not to believe. So, again, logical reasoning is not something separate from imagination and somehow antithetical to it (as perhaps a certain romanticism might suggest); it directly exploits the imagination. As (sincere) assertion involves belief, so supposition involves imagination. It is widely acknowledged that abduction involves imagination, in the generation of hypotheses to be tested; but I think it is equally obvious, on reflection, that deduction also does. Indeed, we might even say that deduction involves treating premises *as* hypotheses—and this hypothetical attitude is what imagination specializes in.[4]

Meaning

Sentences represent possibilities. Their doing so is what their meaning consists in. Meaning and modality are essentially connected. To understand a sentence is to know the possibility it represents. The possibility a sentence represents is its truth condition—under what possible conditions the sentence would be true.[1] The sentence "Snow is black" represents the possible state of affairs of snow's being black, and when you understand that sentence, you know that it is true under these possible conditions. The truth condition of a sentence is simply the possibility that would be actualized if the sentence were true. We grasp this truth condition by knowing the meaning of the terms in the sentence and how they are syntactically put together. So we have a compositionally based grasp of the possibility represented by the sentence; we work out what that possibility is on the basis of the words occurring in the sentence and the way they are assembled.

I mean what I have just said to be familiar and widely accepted.[2] In any case, it is not my business here to argue for this view of meaning; I am going to assume it in what follows. My concern is to show how meaning, so conceived, connects to the imagination. I have emphasized the role of possibility in constituting meaning in order to invite a direct connection—since possibilities are what the imagination trades in. The faculty of mind that represents possibilities is the (cognitive) imagination; so grasp of meaning calls upon that faculty. In the *Tractatus* (which I was consciously mimicking) we find Wittgenstein writing, "A proposition is a model of reality as we imagine it" (4.01), and of course he also holds that "To understand a proposition means to know what is the case if it is true" (4.024). There are three themes here: the picture theory of meaning; the constitutive connection between meaning and possibility; and the role of imagination in representing possibilities. The first two have been very widely discussed, but the third seldom receives any serious attention. Wittgenstein also employs the concept of imagination in this remark: "If I can imagine objects combined in states of affairs, I cannot imagine them excluded from the *possibility* of such combinations" (2.0121). So his thought is that imagination is the faculty that enables us to *combine* objects into possible states of affairs; it is, as it were, modally generative. And since it is also the faculty we use to represent how the world is if a sentence is true, its combinatorial powers will be deployed in that context too. A sentence will contain terms referring to objects and properties, and we use our imagination to envisage new combinations of these objects and properties into possible states of affairs. For example, when I understand "Snow is black," I imaginatively combine snow and blackness into the possibility that snow is black: I envisage that possible combination; I entertain it, I conceive of it. My knowledge of the sentence's truth condition is based on such imaginative acts. To grasp the meaning of a sentence, then, I must *use my imagination*. This is the faculty that is recruited by linguistic understanding. Semantics is accordingly up to its neck in acts of imagining (I could have called this chapter "Truth, Meaning, and Imagination").[3] I intend in this chapter to defend this view, which I expect will strike the reader as shocking and platitudinous by turns. Haven't we got beyond the image theory of meaning? Didn't the later Wittgenstein himself refute any such theory? And yet isn't it a truism to say that understanding a sentence is conceiving of the possible condition that would make it true?

Let us begin by comparing this view to a doctrine of Russell's, famously expressed as follows: "Every proposition which we can understand must be composed wholly of constituents with which we are acquainted."[4] The term "acquaintance," of course, is Russell's name for the faculty that puts us into direct cognitive contact with elements of reality—particulars and universals. It is modeled on sensory perception, with sense-data taken as the paradigm objects of acquaintance. It is *not* an exercise of imagination; there is no envisaging of possibilities involved in acts of acquaintance. This raises the question of what Russell thinks is the name of the faculty that enables us to represent the possible states of affairs expressed by sentences: is it still "acquaintance"? It is hard to answer this question, because Russell does not, unlike Wittgenstein, work with a modally rich conception of sentence meaning; so he does not introduce imagination as the faculty needed to apprehend a sentence's truth condition. But I strongly suspect that Russell is implicitly assuming that acquaintance will suffice to generate an understanding of sentences: once we are acquainted with the reference of each sentence constituent, our knowledge of its meaning will take care of itself.[5] Wittgenstein's insight was that this is not so, since we need to take the further step of *imaginatively combining* the entities with which we are acquainted, and this requires a wholly new mental act—an act of imagination.[6] We need acquaintance with terms at the sub-sentential level *and* we need imagination at the sentential level; and this second component of understanding is a different *kind* of mental act, for imagination is not a type of acquaintance. Imagining that p is not a special case of perceiving that p, since it is not a type of *perceiving* at all.

It is easy for Russell to miss this because he is prone to a mereological conception of states of affairs: he tacitly takes it that the whole sentence refers to the entity that is the complex of each of the entities that are severally referred to by the constituents of the sentence. That is, he assumes that this complex entity is just a *compound* of the objects of acquaintance—and since we are acquainted with these parts, we must *ipso facto* be acquainted with the whole they compose. So sentence meaning takes care of itself; all the work has already been done by the several acts of acquaintance that correspond to understanding each term in the sentence. But as soon as we rid ourselves of this mereological way of thinking, we see that Wittgenstein is onto something important, namely that acquaintance will not take us as far as possibility—and possibility is where meaning has its roots. We need imagination to make the transition from acquaintance with actual things to grasp of a mere possibility—a non-actual combination of objects of acquaintance. Meaning takes us beyond the actual, but acquaintance is tied to the actual. Russell's "fundamental principle" is, admittedly, formulated only as a necessary condition of sentence understanding, not as a sufficient condition; but his entire discussion makes no allowance for the richer modal picture sketched by Wittgenstein. We must imagine the state of affairs a sentence "depicts," *as well as* have acquaintance with the objects and properties denoted by the terms in the sentence.[7] And this marks a large conceptual difference in terms of how linguistic understanding is to be characterized: with an essential use of the concept of imagination or without.

I must now enter an important disclaimer: my thesis is *not* that understanding a sentence consists in conjuring up an *image*—that is, in an exercise of sensory imagination. It is, rather, that the cognitive imagination is employed in understanding, and this is not essentially imagistic (as I explained in Chapter 10). I have no desire to resurrect the image theory of concepts; my claim is rather that imagining-that is implicated in the grasp of meaning. Once this distinction is made, Wittgenstein's own later opposition to the image theory of meaning is not clearly relevant to the theory I am deriving from the *Tractatus*. The following remark from the *Investigations* might look like a decisive rejection of the early Wittgenstein by the later: "It is no more essential to the understanding of a proposition that one should imagine anything in connection with it, than that one should make a sketch from it."[8] But this is cast into doubt if we read this remark as repudiating an image theory of understanding and not an imagining-that theory; and the talk of a *sketch* suggests the former, not the latter. There is nothing essentially pictorial about cognitive imagining, nor even sensory; it is an exercise of concepts, a propositional attitude. So we should not reject the imagination theory on the grounds that the image theory is wrong. The image theory is really a misformulated and oversimplified version of an essentially correct idea—that the imagination is essentially implicated in the grasp of meaning. By not distinguishing imaging from imagining-that, earlier theorists thought they had to maintain that for any act of understanding there must be a corresponding mental image; but this is not a commitment of the view that grasp of meaning recruits the faculty of cognitive imagination. Understanding a sentence is entertaining a possibility, not forming an image of something. This way of looking at the old debate has the merit of finding some truth behind the image theory, though that truth was badly formulated; it is not that the image theorists had a theory that was not even *near* to being true.[9]

It is helpful to divide linguistic understanding into a conventional and a non-conventional component. When we understand the meaning of words, we are exploiting our knowledge of certain conventions—pairings of sound and meaning that are essentially arbitrary. This knowledge is obviously stored in long-term memory and constitutes our competence in a particular language. But in addition to this we must employ another cognitive system, which does not involve knowledge of conventions: our ability to envisage possibilities by means of constructing novel combinations of objects and properties. This task is still waiting to be performed once all the knowledge of conventions has been brought to bear on a sentence. The linguistic conventions take the mind to the objects and properties referred to, but then the mind has to combine those objects and properties into a possible state of affairs.[10] So understanding is memory plus imagination—memory of what words conventionally mean, and imagination of what possibility the sentence represents. This second component will be constant across languages, so that speakers of different languages will perform the same mental act; only the first mental act will vary. We all have to perform the act of imagining the possibility that snow is black in understanding a sentence that means that snow is black, despite the variations in the way this is conventionally expressed. Knowledge of the conventions of language is therefore not enough to deliver linguistic understanding. And since knowledge of the meaning of a word must include an appreciation of how it can combine with other words to form complete sentences, the imagination is also involved in the understanding of word meaning: the speaker must be able to imagine how the denoted entity can combine with other entities to form possible states of affairs.[11] (We should not, however, think that the two mental components occur in temporal sequence; the distinction is a conceptual one.)

Wittgenstein makes a suggestive remark here: "In a proposition a situation is, as it were, constructed by way of experiment" (4.031). The sentence can be compared to a *hypothesis:* it represents a possibility by constructing a way the world might be. We understand a hypothesis by imagining what it says to be true; we understand a sentence by imagining the obtaining of its truth condition. In both cases we are dealing with imagined states of affairs, and perhaps wondering whether they are actual. A hypothesis is a sentence (perhaps a highly conjunctive one); but a sentence is a hypothesis too—even if not always a very exciting or probable one. A sentence is a kind of speculation about how things might be—a possible vehicle of truth, a conjecture. As such it invites an act of imagination. Language consists of a potential infinity of little hypotheses (sometimes big ones), and it takes imagination for the speaker to grasp the import of these hypotheses.[12]

What properties would understanding have if it consisted in an exercise of imagination? First, we need to distinguish dispositional and occurrent senses of "understand": I can be said to understand sentences even when I am not saying or hearing them or am otherwise conscious of them (the dispositional sense), and I can also be said to understand them on particular occasions of utterance (the occurrent sense). This distinction corresponds to the distinction between being disposed to entertain a possibility in certain circumstances and actually consciously doing so in those circumstances. I dispositionally understand a sentence when I *can* occurrently entertain the appropriate possibility upon (say) hearing the sentence; the utterance *triggers* the latent imaginative ability. Since exercises of imagination are active, this gives the result that understanding is itself active; it belongs to our "spontaneity" (in Kantian terminology). And we do of course speak of *trying* to understand, as when a sentence that is difficult or complicated comes along. We make an effort to put the components together and grasp the thought behind the sentence, which may not be easy. In most cases no particular effort is required, but it is still true that a mental *act* is required in order to understand the sentence—even if it is no harder than walking. This becomes apparent when there is an obstacle to ordinary comprehension, as when a perfectly simple sentence is uttered while one is distracted by something else; the mind must double its efforts to construct an expressed thought. In the same way it may be difficult to imagine a possibility, and even when it isn't difficult, an act of mind is still performed. So the active nature of understanding has a counterpart in the activity of imagination. It makes no sense to speak of an effort to see or hear (as opposed to an effort to look and listen), since I am passive in receiving visual and auditory percepts, but it does make sense to speak of an effort to understand—just as it makes sense to speak of an effort to imagine. Conceptually, then, understanding is unlike seeing and hearing, and like imagining.

Linguistic understanding has often been described as creative, combinatorial, productive: we can understand a potential infinity of sentences, and each act of understanding is a small instance of genuine creativity. This seems hyperbolic if one is thinking of linguistic understanding as some kind of syntactic symbol-crunching, a mere following of rules of grammatical construction. But on the richer view of understanding entailed by the imagination theory, such talk seems literally true: imagination is the source of creativity, and it is constitutively involved in the comprehension of new sentences. Moreover, the imagination is the combinatorial faculty par excellence; its facility in producing newly envisaged possibilities is perfectly suited to the generation of new acts of understanding. To understand a novel sentence is to grasp a newly expressed possibility, and imagination is in its element in the production of representations of possibilities. The productivity of imagery is the sensory precursor of such productive cognitive imagination, and it may well be this property of imagery that encouraged earlier theorists to advocate an imagistic view of meaning; if so, they were onto something sound, even if images are not the right imaginative products to invoke.[13] The freedom of the imagination to generate new representations of every kind of intentional object is precisely what language itself exhibits; so it is not surprising if the imagination lies behind the creativity manifest in language use.

The imagination on occasion interlocks with perception, as with imaginative sensing. Not surprisingly, we find this phenomenon in the case of linguistic understanding. I see a printed sentence or hear an uttered one; these are pure percepts, compatible with a complete lack of understanding (I may not speak the language). But these percepts may also be overlaid with an *interpretation:* the words are seen or heard *as* meaning such-and-such. I suggest, not very originally, that this is a case of imaginative sensing: an act of imagination is joined with a percept to produce that peculiar hybrid—seeing or hearing *as.* The case resembles the seeing of pictures: the representational properties of the picture are grasped by the imagination, triggered by the senses. In the same way, the semantic properties of a sentence are grasped by the imagination (acting in concert with stored knowledge of linguistic conventions), with the perception of the sentence functioning as mediator. The resulting psychological state—hearing the sentence with understanding—combines percept and imagination in just the way other cases of imaginative sensing do. This comes out particularly clearly with ambiguous sentences, where we may even switch between one meaning and the other at will. I hear "I'm going to the bank" now in one way, now in another. As with ambiguous figures, the perceptual stimulus admits of rival interpretations, and the imagination has free play with respect to those interpretations; there is subjection to the will in a particularly clear form. The stimulus is passively received in the percept, but it must be actively processed in order to be represented as meaningful, which is where the imagination steps in. When I hear "I'm going to the bank," I can either imagine the possible state of affairs of the speaker going to the river bank or his going to the money bank, and this is what my hearing it one way rather than the other consists in. So, again, the characteristics of understanding are mirrored and explained by what we already know of the imagination.

We are often told that linguistic understanding must be conceived as a "practical capacity."[14] This advice is often motivated by behaviorist inclinations, in which case we need not take it; but there does seem to be a good sense in which understanding is an *ability*. But an ability to do *what*? The usual answer is that it is an ability to verify the sentence or falsify it—or do something else to its truth-value. I won't go into criticism of this view here, though it is relevant to note that the view runs into obvious problems with the understanding of sentences that the speaker has no means to verify or falsify. I want to suggest an alternative ability: the ability to imagine the appropriate state of affairs. This is a purely mental ability, the ability to perform a certain type of mental act; there is nothing behavioristic about it (this is a virtue, not a failing). It is a mental ability like the ability to generate a hypothesis to explain the experimental data, or the ability to perform mental scanning of the objects of one's images, or the ability to daydream. In the case of meaning, it is the ability to imagine the relevant possibility. Without this ability, understanding would not be possible, since we need a way to represent alternatives to the actual—and imagination is what makes this possible. I think this ability is *intrinsic* to understanding in the way that other abilities are not—like the ability to verify. The imagination tells you *what* you are verifying—what possible state of affairs you are finding evidence for or against. It is constitutive of understanding. The ability to verify the sentence or to speak relevantly or to make inferences is a consequence of the basic grasp of the sentence's truth condition, and this is a possibility envisaged by the imagination. Of course, this type of ability will not satisfy those who yearn for something more reductive or observable, but I am not trying to meet their expectations; I am pointing out that we can specify a "practical capacity" of another type, thus granting a grain of truth in their insistence on producing something that connects with action—though with *mental* action. To understand a sentence requires an ability to perform a mental act—and isn't this exactly what we ought to expect?[15]

Chomsky long ago made the point that linguistic use is "stimulus free"—that is, it is not elicited by some ambient stimulus in the manner of a conditioned reflex.[16] We can clearly speak of distant and absent objects, of the nonexistent, the past, the future, and so on. An utterance is not an automatic response to some environmental contingency. In this respect it is nothing like a percept, which is emphatically *not* stimulus free. But of course stimulus freedom is what the imagination specializes in: absence, nonexistence, revision, outright invention. We might even say that the whole point of the imagination is to escape the domination of the stimulus—to transcend the present (temporally and spatially). Imagination frees up the mind to escape what is impinging on it. It is, indeed, part of what makes us free agents.[17] So the stimulus freedom characteristic of language is nicely captured by introducing imagination into the heart of understanding.

Finally, I want to observe that connecting imagination to meaning expands our conception of what meaning comprises: the language faculty is now firmly embedded in the imagination faculty, with all that this implies. The language faculty shares the faculty already employed in imagery, dreaming, belief formation, theory construction, and so on. It is not some isolated module, with no essential connection to other systems; the human instinct for language is bound up with the human instinct for imagination. That is, the semantic component of the language faculty is inextricably linked with the imaginative faculty.[18] This could hardly be more "mentalistic": linguistic understanding is (or comprises) the conscious entertaining of imaginary states of affairs. It does not consist in a collection of dispositions to respond to appropriate "stimulus conditions" or some such thing.

I must now address myself to some natural objections; not all of these have easy replies. In Chapter 1 I gave an argument to show that concepts could not be images: namely, that concepts can be readily applied to perceptually presented objects, but (following a remark of Wittgenstein's) it is not possible to form an image of the very object one is seeing.[19] This might prompt the suspicion that a similar problem would afflict the present proposal: that you can't imagine what you already know to be true. If that were so, then it would be impossible to imagine the state of affairs corresponding to a sentence that one knew to be true—and hence impossible to understand it. Now, I already raised this question in Chapter 10, but it needs to be addressed again because of its relevance to the present discussion. It would obviously be disastrous for the imagination theory if it applied only to sentences that one did not believe to be true. Fortunately, this worry turns out not to be a problem, once we distinguish implicatures from entailments. It is quite true that *saying* one is imagining a state of affairs that one knows perfectly well to obtain is potentially highly misleading, because that suggests that one does *not* know it to obtain; but it doesn't follow that it is *false* to make such a statement. And I think it is perfectly possible to imagine that p when one knows full well that p. Indeed, I have argued that this imaginative act is *part* of having the relevant belief.[20] I know that the sentence "Snow is white" is true.

That does not prevent me from envisaging that snow is white; I can do so simply by forming the right image.[21] So I can imagine the state of affairs that corresponds to a sentence that I happen to know is true; any appearance to the contrary stems from questions of implicature.

A much trickier question concerns necessary falsehoods: these are sentences that can apparently be understood but that seem to express unimaginable states of affairs—for example, "Colorless green ideas sleep furiously" or "2 + 2 = 5." These are well-formed strings of English, and we seem to understand them, but can we be said to be able to imagine the states of affairs that correspond to them? Those states of affairs are impossible, after all, so how can understanding the corresponding sentences consist in their imaginability? In order to deal with these cases, we clearly need to detach imagination from real possibility—on pain of making the sentences literally unintelligible. Now, that has certainly been said of such sentences, but only backed by a tendentious theory of meaningfulness; in any ordinary sense the sentences seem to be meaningful. What I favor here is saying that we *can* imagine impossible states of affairs—that is, we can conceive of them, know what they would consist in, entertain them. Sometimes we may imagine something and not know or believe it to be possible, so the commitment to possibility is not part of the imaginative act. In the case of impossible states of affairs, we do have an intentional relation to them—we can mentally represent them—and in this sense we can get them within our imaginative sights. The case is quite different with some grossly ungrammatical string, where we have no idea *what* we should be trying to imagine. But in the grammatical cases I think the imagination can represent the impossible states of affairs expressed, since we know what it is we are supposed to be getting our mind around.

We might want here to distinguish strong and weak imaginability: the strong kind implies that what is imaginable is really possible; the weak kind requires only that a (grammatically) coherent thought can be formed—that the concepts can be made to hang together into a proposition. Then necessary falsehoods might be said to correspond to weakly imaginable states of affairs. Weakly imaginable states of affairs can be the subject matter of suppositions, and hence of inferences—as in "If colorless green ideas sleep furiously, then some ideas sleep." And this shows that such sentences express entertainable propositions of some sort. There is clearly something amiss with these sentences—and much philosophical effort has been expended trying to say just what it is—so we should not be surprised if they make trouble for otherwise attractive theories of meaning. We might think of them as parasitic on the strongly imaginable cases, in the sense that their claim to meaningfulness depends on their grammatical resemblance to ordinary meaningful sentences; and they do seem like an inevitable consequence of the fact that grammaticality is a matter of syntax, not metaphysics (syntax being modally blind, as it were). In any case, it would be folly to let these anomalous cases decide the fate of an otherwise workable theory. They are sufficiently odd and problematic that they can be reasonably declared exceptional. I think that the imagination can be made to respond to their content and form a suitable representation, even as it rebels at the task. But it operates nonetheless—for how *else* could such sentences be processed? I prefer this approach to the old Draconian measure of banning such sentences as straightforwardly meaningless. Clearly, though, we have a number of options here—none of them altogether comfortable, perhaps—for ensuring that meaningfulness and imaginability do not come apart.

This last point at least shows that the theory is not trivial, since it has some trouble fitting itself to the data. But it might be said that in another respect the theory is too modest, too unexplanatory, too thin. Doesn't it attempt to explain the obscure by the equally obscure? Meaning is elusive, problematic, spooky: but isn't imagination all those things and more? What progress have we made by introducing one mysterious mental faculty into the heart of another?

What we need is a theory that links meaning with something more solid—like behavior or brain states or functional role or causal relations to the environment or biological purpose. If we are to produce a science of meaning, we make no progress by basing meaning on the imagination; for where is the science of imagination? How, in short, does the imagination theory help in *naturalizing* meaning? My response to such misgivings is resolutely unsympathetic: I simply don't share these reductive and naturalizing tendencies. I think we do better to connect meaning with mental faculties that *mirror* its scientifically problematic character—that are as perplexing as it is. That way we do justice to the phenomena, rather than trying to make them surrender to misguided reductionist ambitions. Reduction can be fine in its place, but not as a matter of dogma; and sometimes the most illuminating account is the least reductive. So I think the "mentalism" of the imagination theory is no objection to it—indeed, is a point in its favor, given the nature of meaning as it presents itself. Meaning *is* a remarkable phenomenon, and it needs to be linked to a mental faculty that is equally remarkable—not reduced to something that cannot match its unique nature. Of course, we can go on to try to explain imagination, or at least elucidate it—as I have attempted in this book—but we should not reject the theory because we cannot make imagination submit to scientistic presuppositions. Meaning is also linked to consciousness, after all, and consciousness is the zenith (or nadir) of the mysterious. I conclude, then, that the charge of explaining the obscure by the more obscure has little force. Indeed, I think the modesty of the theory in this respect is a point in its favor. Theories of meaning have tended to be explanatorily over-ambitious and reductive; the imagination theory is modestly non-reductive. It simply says what is the right name for the faculty that generates linguistic understanding. It locates meaning within the several faculties that make up the mind.

The faculty that yields linguistic understanding is therefore continuous with other achievements of mind. Cognitive imagination is involved in the representation of possibility, and hence in modal thinking; in forming negative thoughts; in logical reasoning; and in belief formation. So understanding sentences is connected with these other capacities. But further, cognitive imagination is itself continuous with sensory imagination, a kind of concept-based version of the same underlying faculty—so meaning is not so far removed from images after all. It might *even* be true that without a capacity for imagery, linguistic understanding would not be possible, because cognitive imagination itself relies on mechanisms and processes that originate in sensory imagination. To be sure, imagining-that is not reducible to sensory images, but it may yet be true that it is an outgrowth of image formation—that it is what happens to the sensory imagination when it goes conceptual. The roots of meaning might lie in image formation, even though meaning itself transcends these roots. Images certainly precede meaning ontogenetically (and probably phylogenetically), and their combinatorial and creative properties foreshadow the (different) combinatorial and creative properties of language.[22] The humble image is not to be despised, despite its bad press in much recent philosophy.

The Imagination Spectrum

It could be said that this book has worked up from the simplest examples of imagination to its most sophisticated manifestations. I started with the humble mental image, passed through dreams, and ended with full-blown linguistic understanding (no word yet on the imagination as used in the arts and sciences and philosophy itself). The transitions from one topic to the next have, I think, been smooth and natural. By way of bringing all this together, and to indicate real continuities, I want to present a kind of diagram of the imaginative mind. The aim is to suggest an ordering of the various types of imagining, which might be interpreted both temporally and conceptually. If you wanted to build an imagining creature, these are the steps you might program in. Nothing in this is especially rigorous or empirically confirmed, but I think it offers a useful overall picture of the ground we have covered and the interrelations between the various imaginative phenomena. So, here is my "imagination spectrum":

Percept . . . memory image > imaginative sensing > productive image > daydream/dream > possibility and negation > meaning > creativity

Let me run over this. We start with the basic percept, untainted by imagination—the impact of the world on the infant senses. At this stage nothing image-like is on the scene. The dotted lines then indicate a transition and an important discontinuity: the memory image derives from the percept, but it is not a *kind* of percept; a significant transformation occurs at this early stage. With the advent of the memory image, many of the distinguishing features of imagination are already in play (those I noted in Chapter 1); a new psychological era has dawned. The subject can now imagine what is not there as well as see what is (this ability is independent of the possession of conceptual thought). Once we have the memory image in place, the way is clear for imaginative sensing, which is the combination of percept and image: a current visual percept evokes a memory image, and the two coalesce into an instance of seeing-as.[1] The productive image is not yet accessible to our growing mind, because it requires creative recombination of elements—and hence a larger movement away from the strictly sensory. We might think of the maturing imaginer as discovering this power to create within himself—a momentous discovery. Now he can generate novel images at will, rearranging the world as he sees fit; he is no longer a slave to the actual. And with the image now liberated from the perceptual prototype, the way is open to the temporal sequencing of such productive images—hence the dream (day and night). The imaginer can now string his images together, both memory images and productive ones, to form story-like structures, which diverge from the way the world is objectively evolving. He has discovered fiction.[2] With this development comes the idea of alternatives to actuality—the idea of what is merely possible. Thus the imaginer enters the realm of the modal, of what might be: the dream represents how things might go and therefore opens a window onto possible worlds. The dream presents an alternative world history, thus ushering in thoughts of the contingent and hypothetical.[3] Negation is bound up with this, because negation operates to generate possibilities from actualities: the (merely) possible is what is *not* observed to be actually so. But once possibilities are grasped, meaning becomes feasible, since sentences represent what *might* be so: meaning is all about possible truth (and falsehood). Now the mind can contemplate an infinity of possible states of affairs, each corresponding to a meaningful sentence, and the sensory has been left behind. And then we reach the final step in this progression: genuine high-level creativity. This comes on the scene once the mind is able to envisage ways the world might be and can manipulate these representations to form novel thoughts. Thus the novelist can construct a fictitious narrative unconstrained by actual history; and the scientist can contemplate speculative theories of how the world is objectively constituted. Alternative "worldviews" can now be constructed, using all the resources of human creativity. Thus it is that the simple memory image leads by stages to the highest flights of creative imagination. First there was that infantile image of your mother's face (or maybe breast); now there is full-grown *Hamlet*.

Let me not be misunderstood. I am not saying that any of these transitions are automatic or follow with the rigidity of logic. Nor am I saying that alternative orderings might not be constructed to bring out other interrelations. I am not even saying that my orderings have to be temporally real. My aim is to sketch a natural and intelligible story about how each of these phenomena might be thought to proceed from the others—starting with the most primitive and building up to the most sophisticated. The progression is certainly not seamless, but I think it makes sense psychologically; it is a way the imagination *might* develop. As the seed gives rise to the mighty oak through intermediate stages, so the memory image is the seed that initiates a steady sequence of developments—till we reach the marvels of human creativity. Part of my point here is that this last step is not the leap into the uncharted it is sometimes supposed to be; the groundwork has already been laid in other manifestations of imagination. Indeed, from a loftier perspective, the big break occurred much earlier—when the image made its first appearance. The step from percept to image really is a qualitative leap (*pace* Hume), introducing a fundamentally new phenomenon into the mind. Even the elementary memory image is "creative" relative to the percept that prompts it, since it is made possible only by dramatic mental transformations (particularly coming under intentional control). Once the memory image has taken up residence in the mind, the basic materials for other types of imagination are in place; it only takes recombination to get the imagination started on its journey to the far reaches of possibility. Of course, those later stages themselves require their great leaps forward, and outside assistance from other mental achievements, but we should not underestimate how far the simple image has taken us from its perceptual roots.

The transition from sensory to cognitive imagination is clearly a large one. Up until that point the imagination has worked with materials supplied by sense, though it has assumed a different mental form from that of the percept. But once concepts become the medium of the imagination, we are in a different landscape—in which the liberation from sense has been completed. We are no longer simply seeing with the mind's eye, but thinking in ways that transcend the actual: we are able to suspend judgment and effectively survey endless possibilities. It is doubtful that other animals can do this; in any case, it is a step to another level altogether. But, as I have insisted, it is a step with roots in what went before; it doesn't come from nowhere. In the end, most adult imagination is a kind of fluid merging of the sensory and conceptual modes: seeing in the mind's eye becomes embedded within conceptual exercises that expand the scope and influence of the imaginative faculty. Imagining-that is intertwined with the production of sensory images. The sensory image gives the imagination body, while the cognitive imagination gives fresh significance to the image. Thus when I form an image of a certain person, a whole complex of thoughts may come with that image—thoughts that represent the possibilities I associate with the imaged person. The imagination spectrum has met at both ends, so to speak. I might even write a novel based on my memory images, in which case creativity and memory imagery will have joined forces.[4]

What has I hope become clear is that the imagination is a ubiquitous and central feature of mental life. It pervades nearly every mental operation. It never rests, day and night. The imagination is not some idle luxury or epiphenomenal sideshow, a way to pass the time on a slow afternoon. It plays a constitutive role in memory, perception (seeing-as), dreaming, believing, meaning—as well as high-level creativity. We use our imaginative faculty all the time. Without it life would be a lot less interesting (to put it mildly). Imagination needs to be given more credit in any account of the human mind. In this book I have tried to give it the recognition it deserves.[5]

Notes

INTRODUCTION

1. For a comprehensive and solid survey of the history of thinking about imagination, see Brann, *The World of the Imagination.*
2. I recently saw a television special about our prehuman ancestors in which it was proposed that the reason we survived and other hominid species did not was our power of imagination. This is an arresting thought, which would make our imagination the key to our very survival—not to mention our civilization. Imagination: the greatest evolutionary discovery since warm blood (though doubtless also the source of much danger).

1 IMAGES AND PERCEPTS

1. Hume, *Treatise,* 49.
2. Ibid., 50.
3. Ibid., 51.
4. Ibid., 9.
5. Compare Berkeley, *The Principles of Human Knowledge,* sec. 30: "The ideas of Sense are more strong, lively, and distinct than those of the Imagination; they have likewise a steadiness, order, and coherence, and are not excited at random, as those which are the effects of human wills often are." Also, from *Three Dialogues between Hylas and Philonous,* 225–226: "The ideas formed by the imagination are faint and indistinct; they have besides an entire dependence on the will. But the ideas perceived by sense, that is, real things, are more vivid and

clear, and being imprinted on the mind by a spirit distinct from us, have not a like dependence on our will."

6. Clearly, no appeal to the *detail* of a percept will work either, since some images are far more detailed in content than some percepts; so it cannot be vividness *of detail* that makes the difference.

7. Here we may recall Hume's comparable insouciance about the missing shade of blue: he produces a straight counterexample to his own most basic principle and then proceeds with the principle anyway: "the instance is so particular and singular, that 'tis scarce worth our observing, and does not merit that for it alone we should alter our general maxim." Hume, *Treatise*, 54.

8. So far as I know, Wittgenstein never explicitly cites imagery as an example of misguided conceptual assimilation, but it is about the best example I have come across. I certainly accepted Hume's criterion as obvious when I first read it, regarding it as self-evident; it came as a shock to realize how wrong it really is. The case illustrates how easily our concepts can play tricks on us.

9. Wittgenstein, *Zettel*, sec. 621.

10. Ibid., sec. 633.

11. Ibid., sec. 637.

12. See Williams, "Deciding to Believe."

13. Is visual imagery then better described as a kind of looking than seeing, since this captures its willed character? We look with the mind's eye, as we look with the body's eye. Yet we don't talk this way. For my purposes, either way of talking serves. In the case of the mind's eye, there is really no distinction between seeing and looking, since all such seeing is subject to the will.

14. The subject of imagery has scarcely featured in action theory, along with mental actions in general; I think it deserves serious study within the philosophy of action.

15. O'Shaughnessy, *The Will*.

16. We should not neglect those images that, as we say, just "pop into the head," unbidden and sometimes unwanted. They are not originated by an intention, but they are still *subject* to the will in respect of their course and termination. Causation issuing from the will can in principle get a grip on them—unlike ordinary perceptions.

17. Berkeley recognized this point long ago: see note 5. For further discussion, see Budd, *Wittgenstein's Philosophy of Psychology*, chap. 5; and O'Shaughnessy, *Consciousness and the World*, chap. 11.

18. So it is not that we notice that a mental item is an image and then infer that it can be willed; rather, our classifying it as an image depends on awareness that it can be willed. Not that there are no other criteria we use to identify something as an image; see the rest of this chapter.

19. This is hard to articulate with any precision, but the lability and fleetingness of images is suggestive of their willed character; their "lightness" goes with the vagaries of volition. Then, too, they often contain aspects redolent of desire—the mark of the will. Images present themselves as puppets of volition, if I may speak metaphorically— as if built for intentional control and manipulation. The fingers are likewise built for the will, unlike, say, the back of the head.

20. Wittgenstein, *Zettel*, sec. 621.

21. Ibid., sec. 627.

22. Ibid., sec. 632.

23. Sartre, *The Psychology of Imagination*, 10.

24. Ibid., 10.

25. Ibid., 12.

26. This is most obviously true for the productive image, the kind that results from creative combinations of elements; but it is also true that memory images cannot add to what is already in one's cognitive store. I should also note that the thesis of non-informativeness applies to the *actual* properties of objects, not their *modal* properties. The idea is that I cannot (newly) inform myself of the actual properties of an object just by imagining it, though I may be able to use my imagery to figure out what properties it *could* have. Imagery is not a faculty whereby the actual properties of things freshly reveal themselves; it is essentially reproductive or fictitious. Thus, entertaining an image does not induce the attitude of eagerly awaiting what the world might disclose, as objects offer up their hitherto unknown properties.

27. See Kosslyn, *Image and Brain*, esp. chap. 10.

28. This is why objective changes in the object imagined have no impact on one's current image of it—as they obviously do for perception. Imagery does not involve *ongoing* causal interaction between object and mental state. Of course, one's imagery might contain all sorts of information about one's own desires, personality, and so on, so that psychological knowledge may be derived from it; but it's no good for doing objective physics and history, to put it crudely. You have to use perception if you want to gain empirical information about the world. Images are not *investigative*.

29. The memory image does invite belief, but only because of its invocation of an earlier percept; and anyway it does not invite belief in the *current* state of things—unlike perception. Only because memory images have perceptual prototypes can they give rise to memory knowledge.

30. Of course, I may have *beliefs* about the location of objects I am imagining, but the image does not intrinsically specify any such location. The visual field, by contrast, indicates precisely where in (egocentric) space the objects of vision are located; it needs no belief supplementation to contain such information.

31. Even the most perceptually based memory image exhibits this kind of selectivity—the abstracting of the imaged object from its contingent surroundings. Perceptual hallucinations, by contrast, are unselective in just the way veridical percepts are. The mental deletion characteristic of images is one of their most marked characteristics, and is an aspect of their inherent creativity. Less is more, in a sense. On the differences between hallucinations and images, see Casey, "Comparative Phenomenology of Mental Activity," which makes a number of the same points I make in the text. See also his astute study *Imagining: A Phenomenological Study*, esp. pt. 3, which I came upon rather late in my own research. See also Warnock, *Imagination*, pt. 4, "The Nature of the Mental Image." On the differences between mental images and after-images, see James, *The Principles of Psychology*, chap. 17.

32. See Casey, *Imagining*, esp. chap. 5.

33. Is this why recent philosophy of mind has neglected the traditional topic of images? Perhaps; also, the necessary reliance on phenomenological investigation seems shady to those impressed by behaviorism and cognitive science. I am all for using any method I can think of—and introspection is still the best route to the nature of imagery, I believe (of course, I don't mean to its sub-personal mechanisms).

34. See Armstrong, "What Is Consciousness?"

35. The whole subject of intentionality and attention has not been investigated sufficiently. How basic is attention to intentionality? Could there be creatures with intentionality but no faculty of attention? How important is the voluntariness of attention to intentionality? How do attentive and pre-attentive intentionality differ? Is the attentive character of the intentionality of thought something superadded onto a preexisting intentionality or is it constitutive? And so on.

36. See O'Shaughnessy, *Consciousness and the World*, 486.
37. See Dretske, "Conscious Experience."
38. Sartre, *The Psychology of Imagination*, 16.
39. No doubt this could encourage Cartesian speculations about the dis-
embodied nature of the imaginative mind, as distinct from the perceiving mind; but I don't think we should go that way. The "disembodi-
ment" I speak of in the text is entirely at the level of intentionality—
how things seem, not how they really are. From the fact that I don't
represent my body in a certain type of intentionality it by no means follows that I could really lack a body and still sustain such intentionality.
40. Sartre, *The Psychology of Imagination*, 10.
41. Note how odd it would be say, "You think you have been thinking
about your mother but really you have been thinking about someone
else"—as if your intention to think about someone played no role in
fixing whom you were thinking of. By contrast, my intention to *see* my
mother could fail utterly—as when someone else steps in front of her.
It is up to nature whom I see, but it is up to me whom I think about
(or imagine)—just as it is up to me which finger I try to flex.
42. Entertaining an image is indeed a *way* of thinking about an object, so
it is not surprising that it competes with other ways of thinking. Percepts, however, are not inherently ways of thinking about things; they
are *accompaniments* of thought. One can certainly see many things
one is not then thinking about, but not so images.
43. We can say the same thing about thoughts: there is the perceptual
stream and there is the concurrent thought stream (where this latter
stream joins with the imagistic stream). There is nothing occlusive
about thought with respect to perception! In the case of imagery we
have two *sensory* streams, not merely a cognitive and a sensory; seeing
and visualizing can both flow simultaneously and independently.
44. This is quite a remarkable phenomenon: from being utterly resistant
to the will, the percept is transformed into a plaything of the will. Thus
we are enabled to take charge of our sensory life. The wonder is that
percepts retain their sensory identities through this drastic transformation: it is that very percept I experienced yesterday that now comes
back to me in the shape of a memory image—only now no longer a
percept at all.
45. See Pylyshyn, "The Imagery Debate."
46. See Budd, *Wittgenstein's Philosophy of Psychology*, 110, for this suggestion. The matter is difficult, however, because we clearly can perceive

of perceptual representation—as if the two types of experience attract and cling to rather than repel each other.

6. For further discussion, see Budd, *Wittgenstein's Philosophy of Psychology*, chap. 4; O'Shaughnessy, *Consciousness and the World*, chap. 13; Scruton, *Art and Imagination*, chaps. 8 and 9; Strawson, "Imagination and Perception"; Wollheim, *Art and Its Objects*, secs. 11–14.

7. This joining of imagistic and perceptual space is particularly perplexing: see the next chapter on the space of imagery. The intentional object of the image fuses with the object located by the percept, as if the objects of imagination have come down to earth temporarily—jumped spaces, as it were. (I know this is very obscure, but someone has to say it.)

8. The imagined aspect itself is not updated by the stimulus, though the percept may be if the stimulus changes. If the aspect changes in consequence, that is a matter of what the imaginer brings to the encounter, not what the stimulus itself offers up. A change of aspect is not a change *in* the perceived stimulus. That is the whole point. I am not on tenterhooks waiting to see whether the *stimulus* changes from duck to rabbit; I do not adopt the attitude of an observer toward a change of aspect—any more than when I go from one pure image to another.

9. We might say that seeing-as is imaginative *because* it conflicts with concurrent images: the test of whether a given perception involves an imaginative infusion is whether the subject can conjure up a concurrent image. This, of course, makes most perception non-imaginative.

10. The imagined aspect contrasts with both hallucination and after-image (as well as veridical perception) in this respect. In the case of an after-image, the experienced color, say, really is located in a part of one's visual field, as a real and distracting presence; but the imagined aspect is experienced as coming from the subject, as a kind of interpretation or projection. Still, the matter is tricky, since seeing-as has a kind of *quasi*-locating character: it is as if the imaged object has assumed the *body* of a located particular, without actually becoming one.

11. I know my interpretation of things with first-person authority; hence I know incorrigibly under what aspect I am seeing something. There is no objective aspect of the stimulus that might not match the interpretation I place on it—as if it really *is* a picture of a duck, not a rabbit. Put differently, the stimulus *has* whatever aspect I currently assign to it.

12. This goes against what many people indiscriminately say about percep-

tion—that it always involves an exercise of imagination, because the mind must contribute to the incoming stimulus. But we can agree that all perception is "constructive" in this sense—the retinal stimulation falls far short of the final percept—without collapsing the distinction between imaginative seeing and ordinary seeing. Subjection to the will clearly distinguishes the two kinds of seeing, and it is not to be supposed that all perception involves *imagery*. Using "imagination" to encompass all processes of construction involved in perception simply blurs distinctions—as between my simply seeing the sky as blue and my seeing the reeds in my garden as chickens' legs. Only certain *kinds* of seeing are imaginative in the way this latter case is. Less ecumenically, it is just a mistake to use "imagination" in the broad way many people use it ("the whole perceived world is just a product of the imagination" etc.). And, of course, such usage lends itself to the kind of skepticism about perception as a source of objective knowledge that people calling themselves "postmodernists" go in for. But I digress.

4 THE SPACE OF IMAGERY

1. Wittgenstein, *Zettel*, sec. 622.
2. Ibid., sec. 628.
3. Wittgenstein's explanation is in line with the kind of behaviorist account he is apt to give for mental notions; I prefer pure phenomenology.
4. As, for example, with the kind of neo-Kantianism defended by Strawson in *Individuals* and elsewhere.
5. It also seems correct to say that objects of imagining are presented from a particular perspective—from the front, say, at a minimum. The image also represents relations of spatial inclusion between the object and its parts. If we think of the imagined object as detached from the space in which it originally appeared, abstracted away from it, then we might say that there is still a *residue* of space represented in the image. But an image can never rid itself entirely of space, because the simultaneous features it represents must always be related spatially to one another; there are the features, on the one hand, and their spatial layout, on the other. The image is always "spatially committed"—just as its perceptual counterpart must be—but this commitment is, so to speak, halfhearted. Thought, however, can proceed in a spirit of utter indifference toward the spatial configuration of its objects: an object can be thought to be red, say, without there being any commitment as to its

shape or size or arrangement of parts. Not so for an image of something red.

6. It would be extremely odd to ask *where* the image represents its object as being; and this question is just as odd if we ask it about the "space of imagery," as opposed to the "space of perception." Yet it always makes sense to ask where a percept locates its object, even if the answer is irreducibly egocentric ("a few feet in front of me, slightly above my head"). The image is simply blank with respect to such questions; it maintains a studied neutrality about the whereabouts of its objects, real and solid as they may be (and no doubt *in* space somewhere).

7. I was pleased to discover one other writer willing to acknowledge and discuss this tantalizing phenomenon: Edward Casey (*Imagining*, 53–56). He refers to it as the "imaginal margin" and stresses both its phenomenal reality and its extreme elusiveness.

8. Issues about the non-spatiality of images intersect with Cartesian questions about the non-spatiality of consciousness, and no doubt the former can encourage the latter. When we are told that our consciousness is non-spatial, we might find support for this idea in the phenomenology of imagistic space, and hence for the idea of a quasi-space somehow associated with the physical space of the body. Doubtless this is all horribly confused, but it is philosophically powerful nonetheless. Question: What proportion of pro-dualist sentiment has been generated by (1) perception, (2) thought, and (3) images? In some ways images can seem the most difficult of the three to fit into a materialistic framework, being both "qualia-laden" and yet not as "embodied" as perceptual states. But I won't discuss this further.

5 THE PICTURE THEORY OF IMAGES

1. For a historical discussion, see Brann, *The World of the Imagination*, esp. pt. 3. This book contains a useful and extensive survey of work on imagination, past and present.

2. For this objection, see Sartre, *The Psychology of Imagination*, chap. 2; and Tye, *The Imagery Debate*, chap. 7.

3. See Tye, *The Imagery Debate*, chap. 1.

4. It is no help saying that we "apprehend" the mental picture instead of literally viewing it, because if the image is really a *picture* that we inwardly see, then we *have* to stand in a relation of viewing to it: for any gallery of seen pictures there must be a viewer of them. The picture

theory has a tendency to draw back from the literal interpretation of its key terms, but then it is in danger of dressing up truisms about images as substantive theoretical claims. Thus I certainly apprehend the object of my image, and my image is certainly visual, but this is a far cry from saying that the image is a picture that I see with my mind's eye. And I am simply not in anything like a viewing relation to my image (as distinct from what my image is *of*)—which is not to say that I cannot *introspect* the image.

5. This is just the old homunculus problem in another guise: if the image is seen with the mind's eye, then there has to be a seeing of the image, but this will be an image of an image, which requires a further seeing, and so on. We get a succession of distinct homunculi seeing the succession of mental pictures that result from the regress.

6. See Kosslyn, *Image and Brain*.

7. Kosslyn writes (ibid., 12): "A depictive theory posits a depictive representation (the structure) and an incremental scanning operation that shifts attention across the representation (the process)." His chap. 10 is entitled "Inspecting and Transforming Visual Images." Clearly, the idea is that the attentional processes involved in these experiments are directed toward the image itself as an internal representation. And yet one also finds Kosslyn writing as follows (ibid., 327): "If asked whether frogs have short stubby tails, many people report that they visualize a frog, 'mentally rotate' it so that it is facing away from them, and then 'zoom in' on its posterior quarters to 'see' whether a tail is present." Here the object of inspection is said to be the frog, not the image of the frog. Sometimes Kosslyn speaks of scanning "objects in images," a phrase heavy with the ambiguity I am drawing attention to; as we shall see, this ambiguity matters enormously.

8. So I am not siding with Pylyshyn on the significance (or otherwise) of these studies; see his "Imagery Debate."

9. What images enable me to do is to inspect objects with my mind's eye, as when I form a succession of images of an object from different angles. But I don't inspect the image itself—that inner item—which would require a different mental act altogether. No doubt I can perform this act in certain circumstances, by turning my attention to the image itself in an act of introspection—much as I can introspect my percepts if I choose to. But in ordinary pre-reflective consciousness my focus is on the outer objects of apprehension.

10. Oddly enough, picture theorists don't see that this analogy counts *against* the picture theory: yes, there are deep similarities between image and percept, notably with respect to their intentional objects; but no, imagining is no more viewing an inner picture than perceiving is. Imagining intends absent objects; perceiving intends present objects—same objects, different intentional relation. I can inspect with my mind's eye the very objects I can inspect with my body's eye; it is not that my inspection turns inward in the image case.

11. Sartre insists on this very Austinian point, calling the opposing view the "illusion of immanence"; see *The Psychology of Imagination*, chap. 1.

12. It is not that I have a fixed image which I scan in successive mental acts, as picture theorists are apt to suppose; rather, there is a fixed object that I scan by means of a series of distinct images—just as I can perceptually scan a fixed object by means of a series of distinct percepts. And what would those alleged scannings of the fixed image be if not further mental images—with the regress that results?

13. This increased computational complexity may take the form simply of a larger number of successive images as one's mind's eye ranges more widely over the object.

14. It is known that there is overlap in the regions of the brain that are activated in seeing and visualizing, so some of the same cerebral mechanisms must be involved; see Kosslyn, *Image and Brain*, chap. 1. In no way does this support the picture theory; indeed, the opposite is the case, since perceiving is itself not a matter of viewing inner pictures.

15. Without invoking seeing-as, directed toward the inner picture, it will remain representationally inert—just as an external picture is if it is not seen imaginatively. So the inner viewing of the alleged mental picture cannot be of the non-imaginative kind. Thus the picture theorist helps himself to imagination while purporting to explain it.

16. Percepts are composite too, but this does not prompt an overly literal interpretation of them as pictures of things. I suspect that we use the picturing metaphor for images also because images are of absent objects, like pictures: you don't need to picture what you can directly see. Of course, at least one philosopher has held just such a view of linguistic representation (Wittgenstein in the *Tractatus*), and this type of representation also trades in absence. The picture is perhaps our most

palpable and intelligible form of representation, so we are prone to try to find picturing everywhere—especially when the subject matter is elusive, as with images.

6 WHAT ARE DREAMS?

1. Of course, we must remember that images are not a species of hallucination; see Chapter 1.
2. Though even this may not be as straightforward as it sounds: there might be deep reasons why the features belong together. For example, how could images be attention-dependent without being voluntary, since attention is itself voluntary?
3. The prolonged closing of the eyes during sleep might well be seen as a precondition of allowing imagination its most uninhibited freedom— as if the mind is preparing itself for a long and involved imaginative journey, and will brook no interruptions.
4. It is also true that we don't have disparate *thoughts* during dreams, as we may think of something far removed from waking perceptual experience; this is quite predictable if dreams consist of images but anomalous if they consist of percepts. Dream consciousness has a remarkable unity or integrity compared to waking consciousness—like a single-minded mental faculty operating at full throttle. Waking consciousness, by contrast, is a continual battle for attention, a constant shifting of focus as the senses and other faculties compete for the limited resources of attention. The dream uses up every atom of attention for itself. The dreamer is a monomaniac. Is this why in the dream one has such a strong sense of one's own identity as a unitary consciousness? In dreaming the *I* is always at foreground.
5. I don't of course mean that I can't have a dream in which I am surfing near the Eiffel Tower. I mean, if I am dreaming about surfing in Bali, then I can't then superimpose on this experience an image of the Eiffel Tower; I can't run the two sorts of visual experience simultaneously, as co-inhabitants of my consciousness.
6. So dreams are like daydreams and thoughts: we cannot let our mind wander from them and leave them intact to go their merry way; any divagation of attention is tantamount to destruction. If only one *could* let some of one's thought processes (e.g., figuring out one's taxes) go on automatic while one turned one's mind to more entrancing topics! Both percepts and bodily sensations can be successfully ignored with-

out this ending them, however—which is, I suppose, some consolation when, say, stuck in traffic.

7. I would especially recommend Sartre's discussion of dreaming in *The Psychology of Imagination*.

8. Compare someone who perceives the world well enough but has no imagination; again, such a person "lives" in just one world (maybe most animals are thus modally impaired). Imagination releases us from the perceived world, but it cannot release us from itself—as with the dreamer whose consciousness is fully saturated with a particular imaginative world. Thus we feel *imprisoned* by the dream, possessed by it; it closes down logical space for us.

9. What *is* the unconsciousness of dreaming sleep according to the hallucination theory of dreaming? We can't say that it is the absence of perceptual consciousness, which seems the obvious thing to say. It is certainly not merely motor disengagement, since paralysis is nothing like unconsciousness. The hallucination theory pictures dreaming as if it were just ordinary waking consciousness, except that one's eyes are closed and nothing veridical is coming in. It is, admittedly, hard to say what being awake consists in, but the presence of full-blown perceptual experience seems at least a large part of it—and is normally sufficient for it. The mere veridicality of a sequence of experiences is obviously not sufficient for wakefulness, since you can dream, say, that you are asleep while a crowd is looking at you—and in fact this be true.

10. While unconscious we are not conscious *of* our apparent surroundings, as we would be if dreaming were hallucinating—even though this would be of nonexistent surroundings. We don't have this kind of egocentric intentionality; rather, we have the intentionality characteristic of imagination, in which the body is not the central coordinate (there is no "present-to-me-ness"). The space of imagery is not a space in which *I* am always presented as located, as the space of perception is.

11. Think how bizarre it would be to say, "You thought you were dreaming about your father last night, but in fact you weren't"; whereas there is nothing untoward about saying, "You thought you saw your father last night, but it was someone else." The dream is as immune to errors of misidentification as the image in general is. No one can deceive you into thinking you are dreaming about someone else by adopting a disguise! Nor can you be self-deceived about such matters.

Seeming to dream about X implies dreaming about X, while seeming to see X does not imply seeing X.

12. I often dream of getting into a car for an innocuous trip and find myself facing hair-raising adventures; clearly, the dream is setting me up for an anxiety experience. It is not that such dreams start out with no intention of causing anxiety and then just happen to do so as they proceed; they are designed from the start to lead to anxiety-involving episodes.

13. If we speak of the dream as constructing an imaginary world, then we must regard it as consisting of images, since percepts don't create imaginary worlds (as opposed to illusory ones). In other words, if dreaming is an exercise of imagination, then it must use the materials appropriate to the imagination—images, not percepts. The story-like form of dreams strongly encourages the application of the concept of imagination to them. Of course, we do naturally employ the concept of imagination in this way; I am trying to get to the roots of this— finding a solid rationale for what we intuitively feel.

14. There might even be a rule of minimization for dreams, a kind of Occam's razor of dreaming—incorporate only so much detail as is necessary for the affective purposes at hand—a rule that we tend to follow in other narrative forms (novels, movies, etc.). Ordinary perception is not affectively selective in this way.

15. And if it is agreed that this is a case of imaginative sensing, then it is hard to see how dream experience in general could fail to be imaginative in nature, since the two are so seamlessly interwoven: the hearing of the alarm clock as wedding bells will fit in with the other experiences occurring in the dream. An image has attached itself to a perceptual stimulus—an image consistent with the general flow of the dream. Note, too, how recessive the outside stimulus is; the experience is mostly imagination-driven. The mind has simply appropriated an outside stimulus into its imaginative stream.

16. There is a *continuity* between dream consciousness and other forms of imagistic activity—the imagination manifesting itself at different times and in different conditions of consciousness. The imagination does not sleep when we do, to put it picturesquely. And its activities at different times bleed into one another, as when we daydream and dream about the same thing.

17. Another option is to declare dream images to be super-compulsive, so that it makes sense to try to control them, though it is extremely hard

to do so—like some forms of compulsive behavior. But I think this is stretching it: it certainly *feels* passive to be the subject of a dream, as opposed to being manically and uncontrollably active.

18. This may also be true of the daytime images that "pop into the head." Freud would have thought so. The unconscious has thrown a pebble into the pool of consciousness, no doubt with a motive in mind. The neurotic might be the victim of disturbing images that seem to come from nowhere but in fact can be shown to have their origin in his or her unconscious wishes. Then they are willed (unconsciously) after all, by that other submerged self. Less fancifully, I might find that a recurrent image of someone is actually prompted by my *wanting* to think about that person—though this was not at first evident to me.

19. I am alluding here to the "argument from design"—the argument that we need to postulate an active intelligence to explain the presence of design in organisms. In this case, however, we have the Darwinian alternative—but we have nothing comparable to explain the design of dreams. The design of dreams really does need a rational cause, like the design of novels and so on. See Flanagan, *Dreaming Souls,* for a discussion of dream design.

20. I think they are probably the *basis* of storytelling: the first piece of fiction was a dream report, and memory of our dreams is what first acquaints us with the idea of a departure from actual history. Childhood dreaming prepares us for fairy tales and the like by giving us our first experience of fiction. But this is a topic for another occasion.

21. This raises the question of whether there *could* be a dreamer who was always fully aware of the true causes of his dreams, in whom there was no psychic split and no hidden agency. Such a transparent dreamer would resemble a lucid dreamer—someone who consciously controls the course of his dreams. It certainly does seem possible that an alien dreamer might be thus transparent to himself—as we pretty much are in our daydreams. The question is what would be lost by this kind of transparency: what does the opacity of dreams *do* for the psyche?

22. This touches on the vexed question of why we dream at all—about which I have little to say, beyond noting the inadequacy of what is normally said on the question.

23. The absence of self-location from the dreaming mind is very notable (as opposed to location *within* the dream). It gives rise to an illusion of presence on the part of the objects dreamed about, since these objects are not given as absent from the place *I* am. Perception of the self is

just another of the modes of perception that are closed down during sleep: one is not aware of oneself as located within the spatial manifold. The subject of awareness is no longer an object of awareness.

24. This is the topic of the next chapter—the convincingness of dreams.

25. According to Freud, this view was widely held by theorists who preceded him, with somatic sensation being the main prompter of dream contents; see *The Interpretation of Dreams*, chap. 1. Freud's survey of previous work on dreams is well worth reading and quite independent of his own theories.

26. Such a theory might be suggested by the idea that dreaming involves interpreting activity in the sensory cortex—as if sensation delivers up a series of (possibly random) percepts that are then imaginatively arranged into some sort of narrative structure. Then dream experiences *would* be part sensory core and part imaginative overlay. This does not seem a very plausible theory, however, in the light of the enormous plasticity of dream contents. Daydreaming does not work this way, so why should nocturnal dreaming?

7   DREAM BELIEF

1. Neither perception nor belief is subject to the will; both must fit the world as it is independently of the will. Images are under no obligation to reveal how things objectively are, and hence there is no objection to manipulating them as one sees fit. An image is often merely as one would *like* things to be, and there is no fault in that—precisely the opposite of perception and belief. Truth functions as a norm for these latter, but not so images. Hence believing what one merely imagines is a failure to live up to that norm.

2. Sartre, *The Psychology of Imagination*, 212.

3. That is, with the store of knowledge we carry into the night. I recently dreamed that I was sitting in a restaurant with my cat, carrying on a conversation. I felt nothing abnormal in the situation as my cat spoke to me of everyday matters. The cat was, in the dream, my wife—the cat itself, not my real wife in disguise. I found myself thinking, as she spoke, that we had little in common, and that it was unfortunate that I had married a cat. Other men have human wives, I thought—why not me? The cat carried on chatting, oblivious to my marital concerns. (I had previously been reunited with my cat, and she was being unusually clinging.) Now, clearly this dream violates everything I believe about the world, and yet I was entirely taken in by the content of the dream:

I believed absolutely absurd things that conflicted wildly with what I know very well—with no sense of strain or incredulity. I really believed I was married to a talking cat. There we have the problem of dream belief.

4. The emotion is actually *part* of the dream, as much as the sensory material. It is not that we imagine *that* we have a certain emotion while dreaming, as I might imagine now that I am afraid; we really do have the emotion. If this were not so, we would have an easy answer to Descartes's dream skepticism, namely: I know I'm not dreaming now because I know I am currently having real emotions and these do not occur during dreams. But it is precisely the real presence of belief and emotion in the dream that gives Descartes's problem bite.

5. When I wake up and look back on the dream, I will believe that in the dream I was being attacked by a tiger—but notice that I feel no emotion *then*. So a belief with that relativized content does not lead to the corresponding emotion; then why should it do so *in* the dream? Also, of course, I simply do not employ the concept of a dream within the dream. If I did, we would again have a too easy reply to Descartes: viz., you can tell whether you are dreaming or not by asking whether you are using the concept of a dream in formulating your beliefs. It is the fact that we have the *same* beliefs in both cases that generates the skeptical problem.

6. See Walton, *Mimesis as Make-Believe*, for an extended discussion of these notions.

7. Again, it is not that this idea is totally on the wrong track, as we will see shortly, but it is too crude as it stands.

8. Kripke, "A Puzzle about Belief."

9. So there is an odd asymmetry here: in giving up my dream belief in the light of day, I sense the inconsistency and resolve it in favor of my daytime belief, while in the dream I adopt a new belief whose inconsistency with my other beliefs makes no impact on me. It is as if I totally bracket my daytime beliefs in forming my dream beliefs, but my daytime beliefs are formed in full awareness of the beliefs formed as I dream (insofar as I remember them).

10. It can't be simply that the motor responses would wake the sleeper up, since the emotions don't—and consider sleepwalking. Notice that I am looking for a psychological explanation here, not a physiological one; I want to make *sense* of the dreamer's state of mind (and body).

Clearly, there must be *some* physiological mechanism that causes the sleeper's seeming paralysis.

11. Sartre, *The Psychology of Imagination*, pt. 4, sec. 4.

12. This is the phenomenon Walton sets out to explain (see note 6) in terms of pretense and make-believe. I am not convinced that these notions are strong enough to capture the full depths that fictional immersion can reach—though I have nothing better to offer as a theory of what constitutes such immersion.

13. I intend to elaborate on films and dreams in another work.

14. The child's capacity for fictional immersion is a good model—and dreaming is essentially regressive and childlike. The natural skepticism of adulthood is absent in both child and dreamer; hence the propensity to be sucked in, taken over, possessed, entranced, spellbound. It is as if a work of fiction can take up residence in one's head, commandeering one's beliefs. It is less that one becomes absorbed in a story than that the story becomes absorbed into one.

15. From a certain point of view, the artwork can seem to be engaged in an impossible project: to be the essential stimulus to imagination while effacing itself in the process. The novel, say, is a perceived object that invites imaginative response, but the perception must always inhibit the free flight of imagination. The artwork, *qua* perceived object, strives to minimize itself, to be transcended by the imaginative response it evokes; but of course it cannot expunge itself entirely and remain an artwork. Its very success is its own effacement, yet it cannot disappear entirely from the field of intentionality. The abstract ideal of art, we might say, would be a stimulus with towering imaginative effects yet surpassingly simple in itself—so much so that it would hardly be noticed as it did its imaginative work: a simple line that summed up the whole world, as it were. The tragedy of art is that it can never achieve this, but is condemned to salience and complexity. Art must always draw attention to itself as a perceived object, and hence fail in its highest aim. Art is condemned to be a compromise between perception and imagination. The imaginative end is both frustrated and facilitated by the perceptual means.

16. The idea of self-hypnosis is not, of course, unheard of, as with meditation of various sorts—not to speak of mantras, therapies, and group chanting. (Drugs often play a part in this.) The hypnotist, even when he is yourself, is the natural enemy of the skeptic in you; he endeavors

to break down your doxastic resistance. In the dream the auto-hypnotist can get you to believe virtually anything; you don't always need another *person* to lower your belief threshold.

17. Hypnosis would be the activation of the dreaming mind during waking consciousness, a tapping into the psychic mechanisms that generate dream belief. In some ways dreams do seem the paradigm of suggestibility—the arena in which it works most smoothly. If only Big Brother could recreate the dreamer's susceptibility all the time! Imagine a drug that instantly turned you into a waking dream believer, so that any fantasy or suggestion took immediate hold of your beliefs . . .

18. There is a spectrum of suggestibility, from the persuasive orator or advertiser to the dream itself, along which the threshold of credulity assumes various values, and accordingly a range of different types of unfounded beliefs. Nor is this entirely lamentable, though there are obvious dangers: if we are to share information, and impart useful knowledge to our children, we need to rely on a propensity to believe, even when the evidence cannot be fully presented. It is probably more useful to be gullible than skeptical, at least in the long view, since life without beliefs is impossible. We inherit a disposition to trust one another's testimony without much questioning, and suggestibility is a part of that. When it goes wrong, this is a case of the generally beneficial turning ugly at the fringes.

19. I am tempted by the thought that fictional immersion should be regarded as a *sui generis* state of mind, not a special case of something else, as with Walton's make-believe theory. It is that state of mind in which fictions, acknowledged to be such, take on some of the functional features of known facts, in which imaginative products function *as* genuine experiences; but I find it hard to say anything more illuminating than this. Perhaps a metaphor will say it best: fictional immersion occurs when the work *disguises* itself as reality, while never concealing the fact that it is a disguise. It is as if someone comes to me disguised as someone else, I know this to be a disguise, and yet the disguise is so good that I surrender to it. I let verisimilitude play the role of truth for the duration.

20. Again, we can invert this: there is a dream to the art. That is, maybe art adopts and externalizes the structures and resonance of the dream, suitably disciplined and reconfigured, rather than the dream taking on the character of antecedently constituted art. This would fit the

idea, mentioned earlier, that we are introduced to fiction through the dream, with the dream report being the *Ur*-story. I do believe that the art of film, in particular, relies heavily on the evocation of the dream consciousness, as commentators have suspected since its inception. In any case, there is no denying the visual and narrative artistry of many dreams.

21. Of course, this shutdown will have a physiological substrate, making it resemble paralysis in some respects, but this doesn't contradict the psychological suggestion I am making. The point I am after is that the attitude of fictional immersion makes *sense* of the motor shutdown, since it differs crucially from regular belief and emotion. It is not that in the dream we experience *exactly* what we would if the situation were perceptually presented to us—then we *would* need to be totally paralyzed to avoid jumping out of the bed! That it is only images that are prompting dream belief *registers* with the dreamer, just as the theatergoer registers that it is just a stage in front of her—even though this registering may lurk only in the margins of the fictionally absorbed consciousness. It is not merely a brute fact that the sleeper is immobile, an inevitable consequence of simple unconsciousness; rather, this is to be expected, given the very nature of the psychic structure that constitutes the dream. And, of course, it is simply not true that a sleeping person *cannot* move.

22. This is consistent with allowing—what seems to me true—that the emotions of dreams can attain a kind of purity and poignancy not found in real life, because of the operation of suggestibility and the suspension of ordinary knowledge. The psyche is, as it were, especially vulnerable to emotion during dreams; yet these emotions will not have precisely the character of the emotions we feel in waking life. Emotions, after all, are colored by the psychological context in which they occur. The way that emotions can be accentuated (if that is the right word) during a dream mirrors the way emotions elicited by fictions can attain an unusual degree of piquancy—as with the tough guy who will weep at the movies but never in ordinary life. Fictions, like dreams, can *play* with our emotions, more than real events can—metamorphosing them into sleek and sinewy counterparts of regular emotions. The emotions of fiction and dream are not forgeries of real emotions but their distilled essence. The idea of quasi-emotion is explored in Walton, *Mimesis as Make-Believe,* chap. 7.

23. We might compare fictional immersion to wishful thinking in certain respects. In both cases a lack of explicitness about what is going on is essential to the enterprise: that what is being witnessed is only a fiction, and that the belief is being formed as a result of a wish, not a piece of solid evidence, respectively. Once the nature of the process is consciously acknowledged, the jig is up; it must remain implicit (whatever quite this comes to). So there must be a measure of self-deception involved in both cases. If I am right about the dream, therefore, self-deception occurs there too: we deceive ourselves into taking images as reasons for belief, aided by our increased suggestibility. (Perhaps, indeed, the dream is the original site of self-deception.) Thus in fictional immersion, dream belief, and wishful thinking, we deceive ourselves into believing what we know quite well (though "implicitly") not to be true. Self-deception is a prominent trait of the human condition in general, of course, coming in varying degrees and forms, so it should not be surprising to find it playing a role in these domains. Moreover, the beliefs that result from self-deception are apt to have a distinctive character, not quite the same as regular rational beliefs; there is a kind of shrill insincerity about them, a sort of desperate dogmatism. Thus wishful thinking shares with dream belief the characteristic of being not quite the genuine article, a simulacrum of the real thing (which is not to say lacking in power). In dreams our beliefs attain a kind of false crescendo, a momentary glare that betrays their irrational origins; they are a little bit *too* pressing, intemperate, and impervious. It is not that dream beliefs are held with less subjective conviction than regular beliefs; it is that they are a qualitatively different type of belief—as I think the beliefs of wishful thinking are. And it is not at all surprising that their very different etiology should leave a mark on their intrinsic character.

8 DELUSION

1. Hume, *Treatise*, 172.
2. So there are characteristically *two* defects of belief formation in madness: allowing imagination to shape belief, and not allowing perception its customary belief-generating role. There is a switch from the customary rational mode of belief formation to the irrational method of believing the products of imagination. Of course, it is entirely possible that only one of these dislocations occurs, or one occurs more sys-

tematically than the other. Together they constitute a radical break with reality.

3. It is standard to use the vaguely defined term "hallucination" to classify the pathology of the deluded, but since this term is not expressly confined to non-veridical perceptual presentations, it is hard to know how to take it. I rather doubt that those who use the term understand it in the precise way I understand here, i.e., objectless percept. It is not that the psychotic is being said to be literally like a brain in a vat! Rather, the term is being used loosely.

4. Sartre makes much (perhaps too much) of this in his discussion of insanity in *The Psychology of Imagination*, pt. 4, sec. 3.

5. Jaspers, *General Psychopathology*, 1:68. It seems to me that phenomenological psychopathology is nowadays a neglected area, possibly because it does not conform to the "medical model."

6. Ibid., 69.

7. Ibid., 70.

8. It should be obvious that I am not here attempting to give anything like a full account of delusion. That would require far more in the way of empirical data than I am equipped to provide. My aim is rather to show the relevance of the conceptual distinctions I have been making in the course of this book.

9. I take the case of madness to be a test for my earlier theory of the dream. It would be theoretically undesirable to conclude that dreams consist of images that drive belief while madness consists of hallucinatory percepts that drive belief; better to have a theory that unifies these, given their evident affinity. Equally, it would be unsatisfactory to be committed to the hallucination theory of the dream and the imagistic theory of psychotic delusion. Ultimately, I think we must evaluate each application of the imagistic theory in the light of the other applications, to see whether this theory gives the best overall account (as I warned, no single consideration is going to be apodictic). What I am chiefly trying to get across is that, once we have achieved conceptual clarity on the distinction between images and percepts, substantive questions arise about the nature of phenomena such as dreaming and madness—questions it is not always easy to answer. Let me here make a reference to Currie and Ravenscroft's *Recreative Minds*, especially chap. 8, which also construes delusion as a product of imaginative malfunction. Unfortunately, this book came

along too late for me to incorporate it into my discussion, though there are significant points of overlap between it and the present work in a number of areas.

9 THE IMAGINATION OF THE CHILD

1. It is certainly not a given of child development that percepts are initially regarded as warranting belief; maybe we have to learn to trust our percepts, just as we have to learn to mistrust our images. Perhaps the infant is initially a kind of agnostic about which of these to believe; it is not that it is somehow phenomenologically evident to her that percepts are the mental states to hitch her beliefs to. Discovering this is a *task*.

2. The real is what cannot be (directly) willed, since it is independent of the subject. The concept of objectivity thus has its roots (in part) in the notion of what the willing subject can and cannot control. Put differently, the objective world is what is not responsive to desire. When belief becomes detached from desire, it achieves its true destiny—to fit what lies outside the psyche. The concept of reality is contrasted with the concept of appearance but also, and crucially, with what *I want*. The child must learn the painful lesson, written into all education, that the world is not always as he or she would like it to be. Objectivity begins where the will to power leaves off: thus percepts are vehicles of the objective, while images are not. Percepts force objectivity upon us precisely because they are not subject to the will; images indulge us in our happy self-absorbed solipsism. The imaginary world is the world in which we enjoy untrammeled power. The desire for unlimited power is the desire that one's imagination should become reality; thus it is that megalomania and delusion become fused. The very powerful do, indeed, often live in a "fantasy world."

3. The psychic connections between childhood, dream, and delusion were, of course, a theme of Freud's. As I see it, this is a matter of the psychological architecture involved—specifically the way in which beliefs are formed. All are failures of rationality in which imagination comes to control belief. The arrows of causation go from products of imagination into the belief box, instead of from sensory intake to belief.

4. See Astington, Harris, and Olson, *Developing Theories of Mind.*

5. This test could also be used for the psychotic: do they recognize that imagination is not an acceptable ground of belief?

6. Freud's so-called reality principle is therefore essentially the attachment of belief to perception and its divorce from imagination, which follows the "pleasure principle"—i.e., the dictates of desire. Sanity and maturity consist in the proper management of belief in the face of the seductions of an imagination powered by desire.

7. Although I have suggested in this chapter that the child's imagination may shape her beliefs in irrational ways, I would not want to give the impression that imagination plays no positive role in the child's mental life, or that children below a certain age are simply, as a rule, unable to tell fantasy and reality apart. It is just that they are prone to "get carried away" by their imagination. For an excellent discussion of the child's imagination, backed up by empirical research, see Harris, *The Work of the Imagination*, in which the pervasive role of imagination in the workings of the mind is stressed—a theme I am also keen to highlight.

10   COGNITIVE IMAGINATION

1. Descartes, *Meditations*, 57.

2. It may well be that images, like percepts, have "non-conceptual" contents, in the sense that they are intrinsically belief-independent; certainly, they both incorporate "qualia."

3. The elements also combine to form different types of whole: in the case of images, the whole is a quasi-spatial complex, an ensemble of sensory qualities; in the case of cognitive imagination, the whole is a propositional complex, a structure of conceptual constituents.

4. Scruton develops this analogy in *Art and Imagination*, 88.

5. See Williams, "Deciding to Believe."

6. Indeed, as I shall argue, believing that p *entails* imagining that p. Contrast believing that p and hoping that p: the latter surely contradicts the former (at least under the right interpretations), since one cannot hope that p without doubting that p.

7. Beliefs differ from thoughts or thinking in this respect: to have an (occurrent) thought about something, you have to attend to it (the thing, not the thought itself). Thinking *is* a specific way in which attention is directed, a focusing of the mind. Belief, however, like perception, is not inherently attention-dependent; you can have beliefs about things you are not attending to—or else your attention would be *very* crowded.

8. See Chapter 2. We seem far readier as critical philosophers to use

"think" to cover both entertaining and (occurrent) believing than we are to use "see" for both visualizing and regular vision; there is not the same philosophical resistance to regarding the former pair as species of the same genus as there is in the case of the latter pair. In my view, the two cases are on a par, as ordinary language suggests: visual experience is *visual experience* whether delivered by the eye of the face or of the mind (see Chapter 2). But philosophers seem to have a prejudice against accepting that visualizing really is a type of vision—though not the *same* type of vision as is served by the globes that sit beneath the forehead.

9. Is seeing-as the *root* of metaphorical thinking, its most primitive form? Are we metaphorical beings because we were already beings who perceive imaginatively? Certainly, both phenomena involve the appreciation of *likenesses*. I see the pattern of clouds as *like* a face, as I describe the sky as *like* an ocean. The imagination gets its fingers into both perception and sentence meaning, and maybe the latter is a later development of the former. Is metaphor to be conceived as *thinking-as*?

10. I am thinking of a case in which you have overwhelming evidence for p. It is then misleading to say that you believe that p.

11. Consider wondering whether p over a period of time, now assenting to it, now doubting it, finally accepting it: isn't this best understood as a constant entertaining of p, combined with episodic assent and doubt? Analogously, I may utter a given sentence assertorically or non-assertorically at different times, but I still *utter* it both times. Assertion is utterance plus; it is not a form of *not* uttering! I say the same about entertaining and believing.

12. Clearly, then, general disjunctivists are unlikely to agree with me in both cases. I am not here trying to cure them of their error; my point is that anyone who accepts a conjunctivist view of perception and knowledge should be sympathetic to my conjunctivist view of belief. It is certainly offered in the same spirit. Whether we can go conjunctivist one step further down, for imagining-that itself, is a question I won't take up, but I don't want to rule it out (some views of propositional content would encourage just such a conjunctivism, as with "dual aspect" theories).

13. The image detaches its object from perceived space; imagining-that detaches states of affairs from the actual universe. In both cases cognition achieves a kind of "de-centering." If we regard perception and thought about the actual world as *indexical*, then imagination is a re-

laxation of the indexical mode of representation, and hence a liberation from the self as representational coordinate. I see objects as *here;* I think of states of affairs as holding in *this world:* but when I form an image of something, I don't indexically locate it as here, there, or anywhere; and when I imagine a mere possibility, I don't think of it as holding in *this* sector of logical space. In a word, the imagination is not indexical. (This formulation is another way to put the point Sartre expressed with the word "absence.")

14. So I am rejecting a kind of *empiricism* about modal beliefs, to the effect that they reduce to beliefs about one's imaginative acts. Just as beliefs about the external world do not reduce to beliefs about the perceptual data that warrant them, so beliefs about possibility and necessity do not reduce to beliefs about the imaginative data that warrant *them*. When I believe that something is possible, the content of this belief cannot be analyzed by saying that I believe that thing to be imaginable, still less that I have imagined it. Modal concepts are not inherently concepts *of* imagination—though the criteria for applying them may well relate to the imagination.

11 NEGATION

1. For a defense of the claim that perception does not have a negative content, see O'Shaughnessy, *Consciousness and the World,* chap. 10, sec. 4.

2. Ramsey, "General Propositions and Causality," 238.

3. The Quinean notion of reflexive assent in appropriate stimulus conditions as a model of genuine human belief is therefore wide of the mark. The concept of belief is far more mentalistically loaded than that, a much richer notion. The Quinean *ersatz* is really just a behaviorist distortion.

4. So we should not think of imagining as some sort of *alternative* to serious reasoning—what the mind does when it is tired of rigorous thought. It is *part* of serious reasoning, even of the most brutally deductive sort. Appreciating the validity of the laws of logic itself requires an exercise of imagination, as when one rejects the possibility that anything could be both red and not red. Even when we run through a truth table we are envisaging the *possible* truth-values of propositions, and this involves us in imaginative efforts. Without imagination, symbolic logic would mean nothing to us, except as arbitrary rules for manipulating signs. (Does the tendency toward a

formalist approach to logic issue from a desire to rid logic of its entanglement with imagination?)

12 MEANING

1. Obviously, I am focusing here on declarative sentences. Imperatives, say, would have obedience conditions associated with them; then understanding them would consist in knowing which possibility would need to be actualized for them to be obeyed. In this chapter I conform to the usual practice of restricting discussion to declaratives; the points will carry over, *mutatis mutandis*, to non-declaratives.
2. See Frege, Wittgenstein, Tarski, Carnap, Davidson, et al.
3. I am here alluding to Davidson's "Truth and Meaning"—a paper not known for urging the centrality of the concept of imagination in theories of meaning. Davidson's Quinean "scruples" would certainly not relish implicating meaning in anything so—what shall I say?—*squishy.* Of course, my aim is to reverse this flight from "mentalism."
4. Russell, *The Problems of Philosophy*, 32.
5. Russell's dictum is formulated only as a necessary condition, but it is clear enough that he takes it also to provide a sufficient condition of understanding.
6. Just as we must distinguish the words in a sentence and the way they are combined, so we must distinguish the objects of acquaintance and their manner of combination into a state of affairs. And clearly the same words/objects can combine into different sentences/states of affairs—as with "loves," "Mary," and "John" (these are different modes of combination, it should go without saying). Mere acquaintance with the denotations of these words will not add up to grasp of a unique truth condition. In other words, a sentence is not a *list*—and neither is a state of affairs just an aggregation. This is why the extra mental act of imagining is needed in addition to the various acts of acquaintance: imagining that John loves Mary is not the same as imagining that Mary loves John, despite the identity in the relevant acts of acquaintance with the entities involved in these two states of affairs.
7. It is the structure of a proposition that directs the imagination in constructing the right possible state of affairs, not its mere constituents considered in the aggregate. Hence logical form plays a critical role in shaping the way imagination operates in interpreting a sentence. What was wrong in the *Tractatus* was the idea that the imagining-that which constitutes understanding a sentence is a kind of *picturing*—as it were,

a *logical* mental image. Wittgenstein implicitly modeled imagining-that on sensory imagining in analyzing its representational powers; other than that, I think he was on the right track. So, let me be clear: I am *not* trying to resurrect the picture theory of propositions. Imagining-that is not a type of picturing, any more than belief is.

8. Wittgenstein, *Philosophical Investigations,* sec. 396.

9. It is hard to understand the *attraction* of the image theory without supposing that it was a poor version of something better, since the problems with the image theory are rather obvious. And I suppose it is easy enough—though mistaken—to construe all imagining as sensory imagining.

10. We could put this by saying that intentionality has two modes that should not be conflated: intentionality directed at individual entities (objects, properties, etc.), and intentionality directed toward states of affairs (as when I imagine *that* I am in Hawaii). The latter kind works very differently from the former, and is not a special case of it. Talk of being "acquainted" with a state of affairs encourages the conflation. Thinking of a state of affairs is really very different from seeing an object. (I know this is painfully obvious, but it is amazing how easy it is to miss it in the heat of theory construction.) There cannot be, say, a causal theory of the kind of intentionality that takes possible states of affairs as its object (*possibilia* can't cause anything—though of course their constituents can).

11. So Russell is wrong about individual words too: it is not enough to understand a name, say, to be acquainted with its bearer; one also has to appreciate how the name can combine with other words to produce sentences. What this means is that a grasp of the possibilities involving an object is essential to understanding a name for that object, since one has to grasp how the name combines with other expressions to form complete sentences. So imagination is implicated even in understanding a simple name or demonstrative. This has clear implications for the semantics of singular terms, but I won't go into detail about this now. (Somehow the meaning of a name must include its imaginatively grasped combinatorial possibilities: no mere assignment of an object to a name can capture the name's meaning; nor is the meaning equivalent to a mode of presentation of its reference. There must be a "horizontal" aspect to the meaning of a singular term over and above a "vertical" one—a link to other meanings and not just to the object of reference.)

12. Russell's empiricism makes him construe sentence meaning as a kind of reflection or imprint of one's sense-data; Wittgenstein construes a sentence as a kind of guess about reality—a representation of how things *could* be. Russell's conception ties meaning to the actual and perceived; Wittgenstein's conception ties meaning to the non-actual and unperceived. These are large differences. Wittgenstein's view abandons Russell's instinctive empiricism: meaning in its essence is *orthogonal* to perceived reality, because it is bound up with mere possibility—with logical space. But logical space is the natural home of imagination, which is why Wittgenstein invokes the notion—and Russell doesn't.

13. The combinatorial fluidity of images, their propensity to divide and recombine, their extraordinary freedom and fecundity—this makes them natural cousins of meanings. Perhaps it was this power of combination that impressed image theorists most, not so much the sensory content of images. It is the impressive *motility* of images that suggests their affinity to meaning, not their phenomenal character. Just as we can understand sentences we have never heard before, so we can construct and interpret images of things we have never experienced before; we have a potential infinity of images; and all this creativity proceeds from a finite basis of primitive elements. Looked at this way, the image theory of meaning, though no doubt mistaken, sounds like it is onto something sound; all we really need to do is delete the reference to *sensory* imagining.

14. See Dummett, "What Is a Theory of Meaning? (II)."

15. If anything deserves a "mentalistic" account, *meaning* does. Note that mental actions, though anathema to old-style behaviorists, are actually a type of behavior: *mental* behavior. They are something we *do* with our minds. For some reason, mental actions seem to perturb some people more than mental passions, such as sensations—perhaps because they threaten to bring the will into the picture. I also think that belief is best understood as a disposition to perform certain mental actions, namely, to carry out conscious acts of thinking—which is, I suppose, a kind of mentalistic "behaviorism." My general rule is: never use something non-mental to explain something mental—though by all means analyze one mental thing in terms of another. I believe the day will come when people will find it *amazing* that anyone ever thought that meaning should be explained in terms of bodily behav-

ior—just as now it is amazing to think that only recently the existence of consciousness was denied or downplayed.

16. Chomsky, "Review of *Verbal Behavior* by B. F. Skinner."

17. Imagination is what presents the mind with alternative courses of action—the envisaging of possible futures. There is some merit in the idea, favored by the Romantics, that imagination is the *primary* locus of human freedom: it is what makes our overt actions free by offering us alternatives, and it is itself an instance of free action, as we use it spontaneously to create all manner of marvelous mental products (literature, music, science, philosophy, etc.). Certainly, imagination is the most weightless and unconstrained of human faculties, the most fleet and feathery. See Warnock, *Imagination,* pt. 3.

18. To what extent other components of the language faculty, such as syntax, are linked to imagination is another question, turning upon how inextricably syntax and semantics are connected. Let me also mention, incidentally, that it seems to me highly likely that the imaginative faculty has an innate basis, in much the way that Chomsky regards language as innate. Certainly, the capacity to dream is not learned and must be based on innate principles of dream generation. This deserves further study.

19. Wittgenstein formulates the point in terms of objects, but I think it extends also to properties. Thus I cannot form an image of blueness while looking at a blue expanse, though I can form an image of redness in that circumstance. Of course, nothing prevents me from applying the *concept* of blueness while looking at a blue expanse—so the concept can't be the image. It is as if there is no *room* in the mind for the image of blue once it has been invaded by the percept of blue. One might suspect that this is because the cerebral machinery dedicated to the sensory representation of blueness is already being employed to generate the percept of blueness, and hence is simply not available to implement the image of blueness. Possibly so, but then the point would appear to express only a contingent truth, since we can clearly conceive of a brain that uses distinct cerebral bases for percepts and images of the same color. As I ruefully observed in Chapter 1, Wittgenstein's point seems both intuitively correct and yet difficult to explain. One consequence of extending it to properties is that I cannot, say, form an image of a black dog while looking at a black cat; again, this strikes my intuition as correct. What about forming an im-

age of a dark blue while looking at a light blue? How close can the blues get? I leave this conundrum for the reader to contemplate.

20. The case is strictly analogous to saying you believe something when you know it: knowledge implies belief as belief implies imagination—but it is misleading to say the weaker thing when one is entitled to say the stronger. If we state it in the idiom of the language of thought, then the idea is that belief involves an inner sentence that represents a state of affairs, where this sentence may not occur in the mode of assent: there is the sentence in the head representing that p *and* there is assent to it. What I am saying is that this neutral kind of representing is best described as a case of imagining (this is the personal-level description of the sub-personal story about internal brain sentences). I say this for the benefit of those inclined to think this way; I don't think my view of belief is committed to it.

21. What about the case in which I know that "snow is white" is true and I am *seeing* white snow? Then I cannot, by Wittgenstein's point, simultaneously form an *image* of snow being white. But it doesn't follow that I cannot in these circumstances imagine *that* snow is white, since cognitive imagination is not sensory imagination. Indeed, I am inclined to suggest that perception is like belief in that to perceive that p entails imagining or entertaining that p: when I perceive a state of affairs, I simultaneously form an imaginative representation of that state of affairs—I "perceptually entertain" that state of affairs. This attitude is common to both the veridical and non-veridical case, and corresponds to the notion of *seeming* to see; it is what we would naturally say in a case in which we don't know whether we are hallucinating or not. There is a perceptual representation of a possible state of affairs in all these cases. I am calling this "perceptual entertaining" and likening it to the entertaining that goes on in the case of belief. None of this, however, is required by the account of meaning I am developing: we just need the idea that I can imagine what I believe to be true, even when I *see* that it is true.

22. See note 13. Very little is known about the phylogeny of language, but I think it is worth considering the hypothesis that imagery played a vital role in the upsurge of language all those thousands of years ago. The productivity of the image system, its combinatorial power, its creativity, its complex intentionality—all these mirror analogous properties of language. Dreams, in particular, exhibit these features to a re-

markable degree, and may even be described as possessing a "grammar" (a set of specific rules of generation that are quite distinctive). Of course, images are not sentences with syntactic features, so entirely new properties are needed to inaugurate language proper; but that does not preclude the image system from being a *part* of the cognitive machinery that gave rise to language. At the least, the stimulus freedom and productivity of imagery might prepare the mind for the elaboration of language, by enabling it to have the properties necessary (though not sufficient) for linguistic ability. Just consider the parallel ways in which I can now both form an image of a yellow boa constrictor in a baseball cap and understand the words "a yellow boa constrictor in a baseball cap": it is hard to believe that these capacities have nothing to do with each other, and I doubt that the former capacity owes its existence to the latter. Yes, I know it has become taboo to think of meaning by analogy with images, but there may well be real affinities there; we just need to be subtler in our theorizing about them. Would it help if I said that images have *functional* properties in common with meanings, in the sense of more abstract properties that transcend sensory character?

13 THE IMAGINATION SPECTRUM

1. In the simplest case there is a *likeness* between the current percept and the stored memory image, as when a seen log resembles a remembered cat and I see the log *as* the cat—and this likeness itself reflects a likeness between the current percept and a previous percept. This simple kind of seeing-as consists in a current percept eliciting the memory of a similar past percept, as a result of which the memory image attaches itself to the similar current percept. This seems like a perfectly intelligible step; it would be odd if current percepts did *not* remind us of similar past ones. Seeing-as, therefore, is predictable in a perceiving creature with memory images and a capacity to detect likenesses.

2. I mean this literally: the dream is the *source* of the fictional faculty (I intend to discuss this in another work).

3. Upon waking, the erstwhile dreamer can compare the world he just dreamed of and the world he now confronts; this gives him the idea of a contrast between the actual course of history and alternative possible courses. He can think, "This is the way I know my life is, and *that* was the way it might be." Not for nothing have people superstitiously

thought that dreams are real adventures into another world under-taken at night; the notion of multiple worlds is part of their very fabric.

4. As is often remarked, novels work by evoking images in the mind of the reader, of just the type to suit the narrative and affective course of the story. Without imagery our experience of fiction would be greatly diminished. And it is amazing how much emotional punch can be compacted into a single image (as when we form an image of Anna Karenina falling under a train). The novel's capacity to excite the sensory (and sensual) imagination is surely a main source of its appeal (and also of the suspicion in which it is sometimes held). The role of imagery in science is also well attested: see Hadamard, *The Psychology of Invention in the Mathematical Field*. To me this shows that we never quite leave imagery behind, even in the most abstract and sophisticated of pursuits. (I suspect that images play a significant role in shaping philosophical opinions.) Imagery suits our minds very well; abstract thought can sometimes seem like an ill-fitting garment by comparison. We are *adapted* to images; abstract concepts are a struggle. Thus we lapse into imagery at the slightest provocation. The image is our most ancient and natural mode of cognition.

5. I can't help reflecting how neglected consciousness was until recently. Will imagination receive the same kind of belated recognition?

Bibliography

Armstrong, David. "What Is Consciousness? In *The Nature of Conscious-ness*, ed. Ned Block, Owen Flanagan, and Güver Guzeldere. MIT Press, 1997.

Astington, J. W., P. L. Harris, and D. R. Olson, eds. *Developing Theories of Mind*. Cambridge University Press, 1988.

Berkeley, George. *"The Principles of Human Knowledge" and "Three Dia-logues between Hylas and Philonous."* Ed. G. J. Warnock. Fontana, 1972.

Brann, Eva T. H. *The World of the Imagination*. Rowan and Littlefield, 1991.

Budd, Malcolm. *Wittgenstein's Philosophy of Psychology*. Routledge, 1989.

Casey, Edward S. "Comparative Phenomenology of Mental Activity: Memory, Hallucination, and Fantasy Contrasted with Imagination." *Research in Phenomenology*, 6 (1976): 1–25.

—— *Imagining: A Phenomenological Study*. Indiana University Press, 2000.

Chomsky, Noam. "Review of *Verbal Behavior* by B. F. Skinner." *Language*, 35 (1959): 26–58.

Currie, Gregory, and Ian Ravenscroft. *Recreative Minds*. Oxford University Press, 2002.

Davidson, Donald. "Truth and Meaning." In *Inquiries into Truth and In-terpretation*. Oxford University Press, 1984.

Descartes, René. *Meditations and Other Philosophical Writings*. Ed. Desmond M. Clarke. Penguin, 1998.

Dretske, Fred. "Conscious Experience," *Mind,* 102 (1993): 406, 263–283.

Dummett, Michael. "What Is a Theory of Meaning? (II)." In *Truth and Meaning,* ed. Gareth Evans and John McDowell. Oxford University Press, 1976.

Flanagan, Owen. *Dreaming Souls.* Oxford University Press, 2000.

Freud, Sigmund. *The Interpretation of Dreams.* Oxford University Press, 1999.

Hadamard, Jacques. *The Psychology of Invention in the Mathematical Field.* Dover Publications, 1954.

Harris, Paul. *The Work of the Imagination.* Basil Blackwell, 2000.

Hume, David. *A Treatise of Human Nature.* Penguin Classics, 1985.

James, William. *The Principles of Psychology.* Vol. 2. Dover Publications, 1950.

Jaspers, Karl. *General Psychopathology.* 2 vols. Johns Hopkins University Press, 1997.

Kosslyn, Stephen. *Image and Brain.* MIT Press, 1996.

Kripke, Saul. "A Puzzle about Belief." In *Meaning and Use,* ed. Avashai Margalit. Reidel, 1979.

O'Shaughnessy, Brian. *Consciousness and the World.* Oxford University Press, 2000.

——— *The Will: A Dual Aspect Theory.* Cambridge University Press, 1981.

Pylyshyn, Zenon. "The Imagery Debate: Analogue Media versus Tacit Knowledge." *Psychological Review,* 87 (1981): 16–45.

Ramsey, Frank. "General Propositions and Causality." In *The Foundations of Mathematics.* Routledge & Kegan Paul, 1931.

Russell, Bertrand. *The Problems of Philosophy.* 1912. Oxford University Press, 1967.

Sartre, Jean-Paul. *The Psychology of Imagination.* Washington Square Press, 1966.

Scruton, Roger. *Art and Imagination.* Methuen, 1974.

Strawson, P. F. "Imagination and Perception." In *Experience and Theory,* ed. Lawrence Foster and J. W. Swanson. Duckworth, 1970.

——— *Individuals: An Essay in Descriptive Metaphysics.* Methuen, 1959.

Tye, Michael. *The Imagery Debate.* MIT Press, 1991.

Walton, Kendall. *Mimesis as Make-Believe.* Harvard University Press, 1990.

BIBLIOGRAPHY

Warnock, Mary. *Imagination*. University of California Press, 1976.

Williams, Bernard. "Deciding to Believe." In *Problems of the Self.* Cambridge University Press, 1973.

Wittgenstein, Ludwig. *Philosophical Investigations.* Basil Blackwell, 1958.

———— *Tractatus Logico-Philosophicus.* Routledge & Kegan Paul, 1961.

———— *Zettel.* Basil Blackwell, 1981.

Wollheim, Richard. *Art and Its Objects.* Cambridge University Press, 1980.

Index

Fiction, 4
Fictional immersion, 103–106, 109, 111, 112, 183nn14–15, 186n23
Films, fictional immersion in, 103, 106, 111
Foveation, 22
Frame, of image, 59–60
Frege, Gottlob, 143
Freud, Sigmund, 84, 91, 92, 180n18, 181n25, 188n3

General Psychopathology (Jaspers), 117
Grandeur, delusions of, 113–114

Hallucination, 4, 10, 12; absence and, 29; belief and, 21; causation and, 15; children's imagination and, 123; delusions distinguished from, 114, 115–116, 187n3; dream belief and, 99; dreams and, 74, 76, 77, 78, 81, 95, 178n9; drug-induced, 33; imaginative seeing and, 54–55; as percept without external object, 45; pseudohallucination distinguished from, 117–118; unselectivity of, 168n31; wakefulness and, 81
Hearing, sense of, 57, 77, 116, 119, 150
Hegel, G. W. F., 1
Hume, David, 1, 8–11, 36, 161; on image as copy, 34; on madness, 114; on passive reception of image, 16; on percept and observation, 19; on willed visualization and, 12

Hypnagogic imagery, 87–88
Hypnosis, 106–108, 183–184n16, 184n17
Hypotheses, 142, 143, 149, 152

Iconic trace, 35, 36
Identity, of object, 31, 82–83
Ideology, 1
Illusions, 54, 87, 92, 114, 115
Images, mental: absence and, 29–30; attention and, 26–29, 78; belief and, 96, 121; causation of, 15; as concepts, 37; delusion and, 119; depth in, 47; dreams and, 74–88; energy overload and, 24; frame of, 59–60; indeterminacy and, 25; memory and, 11, 34–36; observation and, 17–22; occlusion and, 32–34; percepts and, 2–3, 7–41; picture theory of, 61–73; "poverty" of, 19, 26, 51; recognition and, 30–32; saturation and, 25–26; sense-datum conception of, 68; space of imagery, 56–60, 173n5; as thoughts, 36–39; visual field and, 22–25; will and, 12–17, 85, 167nn18–19
Imagination, 1–2, 6, 29, 151; abnormal (delusionary), 114–115; absence and, 30; beliefs and, 4; of children, 121–127; cognitive, 128–139, 148, 157–158, 162; delusionary, 118–120; diverse expressions of, 5; dream consciousness and, 80; imaginative sensing, 86–87; meaning and, 144–145; necessary falsehoods and, 155–156; negation and,

Imagination *(continued)* 140–143; perceptual distortions and, 49; picture theory of images and, 71–72; possibilities and, 195n17; puberty and sexual fantasies, 127; spectrum of, 159–163; "voices in the head," 116

Indeterminacy, 51

Indexical representation, 190–191n13

Intelligent design, 90

Intentionality, 17, 30, 36, 39, 193n10; attention and, 52, 168n35; dreams and, 178n10; fictional immersion and, 105–106, 183n15; image as vehicle of, 45; picture theory of images and, 71; pre-attentive, 26–27; space of imagery and, 58

Jaspers, Karl, 117

Kant, Immanuel, 1

Kierkegaard, Søren, 1

Knowledge, 138, 142, 168n29; linguistic understanding and, 149, 151; meaning and, 146; observation and, 17–22

Kripke, Saul, 101

Language, 149, 158; imagination and, 153–154, 195n18; learning of, 122; meaning and, 151, 196n22; stimulus freedom of, 153

Locke, John, 1

Logic, 5, 101, 143, 161; cognitive imagination and, 158; dreams

and, 178n8; negation and, 191n4

Lucid dreams, 89, 180n21

Madness (insanity), 2, 8, 10, 99; belief formation in, 186n2; as disturbance of imagination, 114; dreams and, 113, 120, 123, 187n9; as imagination-driven belief, 124, 126

Magnetic resonance imaging (MRI), 108

"Make-believe," 98, 183n12

Meaning, 144–158

Memory: disorder of, 115; fictional immersion and, 109; imagination and, 160, 161–162, 163; knowledge and, 168n29; recognition and, 31, 83; understanding and, 148

Memory images, 11, 19, 34–36

Metaphorical belief, 134–135, 190n9

"Mind's eye," 41, 42–47, 162; dreams and, 74; hallucination and, 54; picture theory of images and, 62, 63–65, 67, 69, 70–71, 73; seeing versus looking, 166n13; visual inspection with, 175n9, 176n10. *See also* Eyes, bodily

Modality, 144

Motor activity, delusion and, 119

Muller-Lyer illusion, 53, 54, 87

Naïve realism, 4, 45

Narrative, in dreams, 84–85, 89, 102, 110, 179n14

Negation, 4–5, 140–143, 160

Novels, fictional immersion in, 103, 105, 109–110, 183n15, 198n4

Objects: absent, 50, 176n10, 180n23; attention dependence and, 27; of dreams, 84, 85, 93; hallucination and, 45; of image and of percept, 57; imaginative seeing and, 54; objective changes in, 167n28; observation and, 19; picture theory of images and, 61–73; recognition and, 30–31; space of imagery and, 57, 58; visual field and, 23
Observation, 17–22, 132
Occlusion, 32–34, 53, 116, 132
O'Shaughnessy, Brian, 14, 171n4

Particulars, 146
Percepts, 2–3, 7–12, 130; absence and, 29–30; attention and, 26–29; beliefs and, 21, 96, 98, 99, 113, 139; causation of, 15; in children's minds, 126; dreams and, 74–88; imagination spectrum and, 159–160; indeterminacy and, 25; in infant's mind, 121, 159; memory images and, 34–36; observation and, 17–22; occlusion and, 32–34; picture theory of images and, 67, 72; recognition and, 30–32; saturation and, 25–26; space of imagery and, 57, 58; thought and, 169n42; visual field and, 22–25; will and, 12–17, 169n44, 188n2
Perceptual distortions, 49
Persecution, delusions of, 113–114

Phenomenology, 7, 16, 171n5; of infant mind, 121; pseudohallucinations and, 117; resemblance of images to percepts, 41; space of imagery and, 58
Philosophical Investigations (Wittgenstein), 48, 147
Philosophy, 1, 6, 11, 117, 159
Pictures, seeing of, 49, 72, 73, 176n10; internal pictures, 64–65, 66, 68; meaning and, 145
Possibilities, 144–145; imagination and, 157–158, 162; meaning and, 149, 151; negation and, 141, 142; understanding and, 150
Presence, 29, 92, 93, 94
Proprioceptive percept, 93
Pseudohallucinations, 117, 118
Psychiatry, 117
Psychodrama, 117
Psychology of Imagination (Sartre), 17
Psychopathology, 117
Psychosis, 4

Ramsey, Frank, 142
Rationalism, 5
Reality inversion, 126
Recognition, 30–32, 82–84
Religious belief, 112
Representation, 69, 129; indexical, 190–191n13; medium of, 63; of negation, 141–142, 143; of possibility, 137
Repression (Freudian concept), 91
Response times, 70–71
Retina, 22, 35, 42. *See also* Eyes, bodily

Russell, Bertrand, 5, 146–147, 193n11, 194n12

Sartre, Jean-Paul, 1, 20; on absence, 29, 30; on dream images, 96; on images and knowledge, 17–18; on "poverty" of image, 19, 26; on recognition, 30–31
Saturation, 25–26, 28, 85–86
Scanning, 3, 67, 69–70, 119, 175n7
Schizophrenia, 4, 116, 119
Sciences, 2, 142, 159. *See also* Cognitive science
Seeing-as, 48–53, 94, 135, 160, 163; imagination spectrum and, 197n1; locating character of, 172n10; metaphorical belief and, 135; will and, 181n1
Seeing (perception), 27, 134; contrast with seeing-as, 52, 53–54; imaginative, 48–55; looking and, 56; "mind's eye" and, 42, 43–44; visualizing distinguished from, 3, 12–13; wakefulness and, 80–82
Sense-datum view, 68
Sense-modalities, 7, 26, 41, 72, 74
Sensory imagination, 129–130, 135, 162
Sexual fantasies, 14, 127
Sleep, 8, 74, 81, 177n3; hypnagogic imagery and, 87–88; hypnosis and, 107; imaginative sensing and, 86
Sleepwalking, 88
Space: computational complexity and, 71; of imagery, 56–60; picture theory of images and, 67;

spatial relatedness, 30; visual image and, 23, 24
Stoics, 1
Suggestibility, 4, 106, 107, 108, 118, 184n18
Superstition, 124
Syntax, 156, 195n18

Theatrical productions, 103, 109
Therapy, 14
Thomas Aquinas, Saint, 1
Thought: dreams and, 177n6; in image and percept, 32; images as thoughts, 36–39; negation and, 141; percepts and, 169nn42–43; will and, 15, 29
Touch, space of, 57
Tractatus Logico-Philosophicus (Wittgenstein), 145, 147, 176n16, 192n7
Treatise of Human Nature, A (Hume), 8

Unconscious, the, 4, 91, 97, 180
Understanding, linguistic, 148–153, 158
Universals, 146

Veridical seeing, 55, 81, 137, 178n9
Vision, space of, 57
Visual experience, 43, 44–45, 78, 171n5
Visual field, 22–25
Visualization, 3, 7, 9, 13, 46

Willed action, imaging as, 12–17, 28–29, 35, 180n18; attention dependence and, 39, 40; child's imagination and, 122–123; cognitive imagination and, 131–132; concept of aspect and, 49; delusion and, 118; dream narrative and, 84–85, 88, 89, 90; imaginative seeing and, 50–51; infant's mind and, 121; meaning and, 152

Wittgenstein, Ludwig, 1, 5, 50, 133, 154; on imagery, 11–12; information flow and, 20; on looking and imagining, 37–38; on meaning, 147, 194n12; on observation, 17; on philosophical error, 11; on propositions, 145, 149; on "seeing as," 48–49; on space of imagery, 56, 57, 58, 59; on the will, 14

Zettel (Wittgenstein), 49